BERLITZ®

KT-379-332

JAMAICA

1989/1990 Edition

By the staff of Berlitz Guides
A Macmillan Company

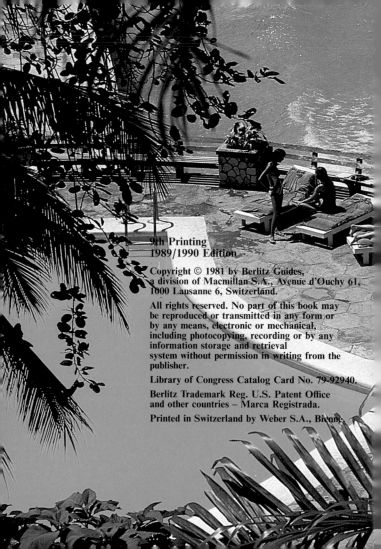

9th Printing
1989/1990 Edition

Copyright © 1981 by Berlitz Guides,
a division of Macmillan S.A., Avenue d'Ouchy 61,
1000 Lausanne 6, Switzerland.

All rights reserved. No part of this book may
be reproduced or transmitted in any form or
by any means, electronic or mechanical,
including photocopying, recording or by any
information storage and retrieval
system without permission in writing from the
publisher.

Library of Congress Catalog Card No. 79-92940.

Berlitz Trademark Reg. U.S. Patent Office
and other countries – Marca Registrada.

Printed in Switzerland by Weber S.A., Bienne.

How to use our guide

- All the practical information, hints and tips that you will need before and during the trip start on page 105.

- For general background, see the sections Jamaica and the Jamaicans, p. 6, and A Brief History, p. 12.

- All the sights to see are listed between pages 19 and 47. Our 🏃 own choice of sights most highly recommended is pinpointed by the Berlitz traveller symbol. Information on sports, shopping, nightlife and the Jamaican cuisine is described between pages 48 and 60.

- Special sections on Haiti, the Dominican Republic and the Cayman Islands with their own summaries of leisure activities and practical information are to be found on pages 60–85, 86–98 and 99–104 respectively.

- Finally, there is an index at the back of the book, pp. 126–128.

Although we make every effort to ensure the accuracy of all the information in this book, changes occur incessantly. We cannot therefore take responsibility for facts, prices, addresses and circumstances in general that are constantly subject to alteration. Our guides are updated on a regular basis as we reprint, and we are always grateful to readers who let us know of any errors, changes or serious omissions they come across.

Text: Catherine McLeod
Photography: Jürg Donatsch
Layout: Doris Haldemann
We wish to thank the Jamaica Tourist Board for their help with this guide. We're also grateful to the Haiti National Office of Tourism and Public Relations, the Dominican National Tourist Bureau and the Cayman Islands Department of Tourism for information and assistance.
Cartography: 🔵 Falk-Verlag, Hamburg.

Contents

Jamaica and the Jamaicans

Christopher Columbus, the first authenticated tourist in these parts and no mean connoisseur of islands, put Jamaica down in history as "the fairest island that eyes have beheld". Back in Spain at the court of Queen Isabella, he crumpled up a piece of parchment as a practical demonstration of how it looked.

Shaped more or less like a turtle swimming west, Jamaica lies 600 miles south-east of Miami, 90 miles from Cuba. It's a big island, third largest in the Caribbean, measuring 146 miles in length and 51 miles across at its widest point.

Jamaica's vegetation, geography and climate vary considerably. At Mandeville, in the hills, you'll sleep with a blanket on your bed. The east coast, liberally sprinkled with warm rain showers from the

high country, has lush, jungle-like foliage—some of the most beautiful scenery on the island. The Blue Mountains are Jamaica's central ribbing, and they often are blue with trailing mists; four of the peaks rise over 6,000 feet. The central plain contains the pock-marked landscape of Cockpit Country, where rain has etched bizarre formations in the limestone. Finally, rimming the north coast, you'll find one superb beach after another.

The island vibrates with colours, scents, sounds and legends. There are royal palms and those ubiquitous coconut trees, now mostly the stocky dwarf variety. There are orchids galore, red-orange poinciana, *poui* with hardly a leaf to disturb the sunshine-yellow flowers and flaming poinset-

Young Jamaicans have a heritage of fine buildings, like Devon House.

tias. Many-hued hibiscus flowers grow as big as saucers, while the bamboo forms veritable cathedrals. Not to mention tender nests of fern, breadfruit and banyan trees. The latter is likely to be inhabited by "duppies" or ghosts, for Jamaica has more than its fair share of superstitions.

All this is orchestrated by the twittering of the island's 200 or so ornithological species—including the shrill song of the kling-kling and the droning of humming-birds—as well as croaker lizards and whistling tree frogs.

The Arawak Indians, Jamaica's first inhabitants, called the island "Xamayaca", land of wood and water. The Spanish arrived in the 16th century, obliterated the Arawaks, but left few traces of their own stay. The British, on the other hand, bequeathed a scattering of "great houses", not always as great as all that, since plantation owners lived mostly in England and their Caribbean residences were practical affairs, notable mainly for their airy architecture. Another legacy of that era: many Jamaican place names—Falmouth, Cambridge, Bath, Warwick and Newport—are English.

So, in principle at least, is the language. Although Jamaicans of all colours speak English with an Irish (some say Welsh) accent, a heritage from the slave days of white overseers, among themselves they are more likely to converse in dialect. This rich soup of English, Spanish and African, pretty well incomprehensible to all but the initiated, is studded with out-of-the-way terms and humour. "Soon come", one of the commonest of these, really means that if you're very patient and don't try to push anybody around, you'll get what you want in the end because intentions are basically good.

The Jamaican personality exaggerates, procrastinates, dramatizes, over-reacts. People are likely to tell you exactly what they think of you. Their sense of humour is extraordinary, irreverent and wordy, for this is a supremely verbal race. You may sometimes think they're laughing at you. Nothing surer. Laugh back.

Understanding the Jamaicans is the key to enjoying your stay. Proud and dignified—their country has been independent from Britain

It may not take long to eat a banana but it takes the plant a year to produce the first bunch.

since 1962—they detest and react strongly to anything that seems to put them in a servile position. The apparent wealth of the tourists makes them aware of their relative poverty. But if you go out of your way just a little, taking the first step in getting acquainted, you're likely to be accepted. Don't overlook the fact that there is a culture here—in art, music and the theatre. It's new and sometimes seems oversure of itself to make up for uncertainties. Not just a mixture of African, American and British cultures, it is uniquely Jamaican.

You'll find all shades of colour on the island, from the

curly-haired blonds with African features on the south coast through coffee colour to black. One thing they have in common, though, is living Jamaica's motto of "Out of many, one people."

When it comes to eating, you can choose anything from **10** a hamburger to a dish called "stamp and go" (fishcakes, really), from international cuisine to plantains and the ever-present rice n'peas (where the "peas" are red beans). You are likely to breakfast off mangoes and paw-paw, chew on a stick of sugar-cane, refresh yourself with coconut water and feast on red snapper. Doubtless,

White sand rims a curve of turquoise sea at Boston Beach.

you'll sample the famous rum or top off dinner with a cup of strong Blue Mountain coffee and a glass of Tia Maria.

Jamaica's touristic infrastructure is excellent. Hotels abound, villas are imaginative, beaches measure up to your visions of an island paradise and there is every sort of sport imaginable, from snorkelling and cricket to dominoes (a national weakness). Just one point: don't go into the southwestern districts of downtown Kingston, don't wander along lonely beaches at night—and don't exaggerate the problems.

Jamaica is also a good base for excursions to other islands of the Caribbean. A 40-minute plane ride can lift you from Jamaica to Haiti, the first black republic in the world, then on to the Dominican Republic, where early American history and Spanish influence can still be felt, or to the Caribbean tax haven known as the Cayman Islands.

In the end, Jamaica is an exotic paradise where you can climb a waterfall, raft down a river, watch the fireflies blinking in the valleys, tremble deliciously at stories of the lascivious white witch, move to the beat of calypso or reggae or array yourself in the latest resort wear to dine in candle-lit splendour. Not to mention those sighing breezes, swaying palms and turquoise seas. Jamaica will enchant, provoke and fascinate. Not bad for an island of 4,411 square miles. **11**

A Brief History

The Arawak Indians were Jamaica's original inhabitants. They probably arrived from South America around A.D. 700. Gentle, primitive and shy, the Arawaks farmed, fished and lived in small villages of thatched huts. They were blessed with abundant food and appear to have been totally nonbelligerent. When they disappeared, the Arawaks left little to the world except some words—"tobacco", "hurricane", "potato", "canoe" and the name for Jamaica, "Xamayaca".

The Spanish Era

Christopher Columbus sighted Jamaica in 1494 on his second voyage to the New World. During his fourth trip (1502–03), he and his crew were marooned for a year at St. Ann's Bay on the northern coast of the island. Most of what we know about the Arawaks comes from the account of a priest who accompanied Columbus.

When the Spanish arrived in Jamaica, there were 60,000 Arawaks. But by the time the English took over in 1655, the Arawaks had disappeared—decimated by imported diseases or killed by their European overlords.

Jamaica's first Spanish governor, Don Juan de Esquivel, founded a settlement at Sevilla la Nueva (near St. Ann's Bay) in 1510. It was never a healthy site, and in time the Spanish moved the capital south near the Rio Cobre to St. Jago de la Vega. (Under the British, this became simply Spanish Town.)

Once they discovered there was no gold in Jamaica, the Spanish took little interest in the place. However, they did plant tobacco, sugar cane and bananas and raised some cattle and hogs. African slaves were brought in to replace the ill-fated Arawaks. For the most part, Jamaica was a stocking-up point for ships on their way to richer prizes in the Caribbean and South America.

The British Take-Over

The British captured Jamaica in 1655. Oliver Cromwell, jealous of Spain's strength in the West Indies, came up with the Western Design. Rather grander on paper than it was in fact, it aimed at control of the Caribbean. He sent an expedition to take the island of Hispaniola (now Haiti and the Dominican Republic). It was a disaster. As a face-saving oper-

ation, the remnant of the force decided to go for Jamaica.

They landed in what is now Kingston Harbour on May 10, 1655. The Spanish surrendered almost at once, headed for the north coast and sailed off for Cuba. The few who remained under Don Cristobal Ysassi were subdued by the British after five years of guerrilla warfare. The Treaty of Madrid (1670) set official seal on England's claim to Jamaica.

The former Spanish slaves, who had taken to the hills in inaccessible areas, hectored the English for many years more. Known as Maroons (from the Spanish *cimarrón*, meaning "untamed"), they were never conquered. The British finally made a treaty with them, guaranteeing certain privileges and measures of independence which their descendants (who live in the Cockpit Country and in the eastern mountains) still enjoy.

Jamaica was to become Britain's most valuable Caribbean possession, and piracy supplied the first riches. The original buccaneers were men who settled in north-west Hispaniola and gained a relatively honest livelihood trading wild pork and beef to the Spanish. In fact, the word "buccaneer" comes from *boucan*, the frame on which they dried the meat. But it didn't take them long to realize that there were richer rewards in booty than beef, and they sailed out in captured ships to attack Spanish galleons, returning home laden with precious metals and stones.

In time the buccaneers **13**

banded together, amassing arms and ships. The sparring European governments were only too happy to make use of them, bestowing commissions known as letters of marque and encouraging the pirates to terrorize the fleets and raid the settlements of other countries. Tortuga Island, off Hispaniola, and Port Royal in Jamaica were their two most infamous hideaways.

In 1692, Port Royal, "the wickedest place in Christendom", was struck by a gigantic earthquake. Most of it simply disappeared into the sea. The island was still recovering from this shock when it was forced to beat off a French attack. Though this was the last such invasion, many forts were erected as protection against continuing threats from France or Spain.

King of the Pirates
Welshman Henry Morgan was the uncrowned king of the "Brethren of the Coast". He set up headquarters in Port Royal, and the governor of Jamaica gave him a commission to attack Spanish ships. He was most successful. But after the Treaty of Madrid recognized England's claim to Jamaica, Morgan no longer had a legitimate excuse to prey on Spain.

He was tried for piracy in London, pleaded patriotic motives and was acquitted. Moreover, he was honoured with a knighthood and returned to Jamaica to become governor. At this point, the brazen ex-buccaneer did an about-face and clamped down on his old profession with all the righteousness of a converted sinner. Henry Morgan died in his bed in 1688 and enjoyed the honours of a state funeral.

Sugar and Slavery

The sugar story is one of brutish subjugation, cruelty and greed. It dominated Jamaica in the 18th century. The early settlers had planted indigo, tobacco and cacao, but it was sugar that brought great wealth. In order to work the vast plantations, black slaves were imported from Africa. Most of them were forced to labour in the fields and later the factories. By 1785 Jamaica had 250,000 slaves, outnumbering the white population ten to one. Payment for them was often made in rum and sugar.

Slaves were encouraged to reproduce, but families were deliberately broken up. This still has repercussions in Jamaica today where the rate of illegitimacy remains very high; children are frequently reared

Fort Charles saw them all, from Lord Nelson to Morgan the pirate.

by female members of the family and society is characterized by strong, independent women. A separate class, the freedmen, were the result of unions between white men and black women. Within the European society, too, there was a separate class, the overseers and book-keepers. The latter were overworked, badly paid and only somewhat less exploited than the slaves. And, to make matters worse, many plantation owners were absentee landlords, living a life of luxury in England.

There was constant fear of slave uprisings. Numerous revolts did break out and these were always followed by cruel reprisals. Non-conformist missionaries who supported the slaves' cause were also subjected to acts of terrorism, including the burning of their churches. The slave rebellion in the parish of St. James in 1831 was attributed to their influence.

Emancipation
Finally in 1834, slavery was abolished by an act of Parliament. Emancipation was to be achieved over a three-year period during which the slaves would work part-time and receive wages from their ex-masters. This system could not hope to succeed. Complete

emancipation came in 1838 and the freed slaves left their old estates as quickly as possible, occupying small areas of idle land or settling in villages. The planters were compensated by the British government.

Then, in 1865, there was the Morant Bay Rebellion, a naïve, almost pacific attempt to obtain justice for the freed slaves. They had virtually no voice in the country, and drought had worsened their already poor living conditions. The British government had ignored one appeal after another. Paul Bogle led a band of freed slaves to the court house in Morant Bay and answered resistance by setting it alight. Some 16 people were killed in the mêlée. Once again reprisals were swift and unjust. More than 400 people—including Bogle and William Gordon, a leading black member of the House of Assembly—were shot or hanged.

Britain itself protested against the inhumanity of the punishments. The governor, Edward Eyre, was dismissed and there was even an unsuccessful attempt to bring him to account as a murderer.

The cane sugar industry is still important in Jamaica's economy.

Late in the 19th century, the development of the banana trade helped the faltering economy. Sugar had, by then, long since passed its peak.

Toward Independence

In more recent times, the depression of the 1930s fell upon an economically backward country with an unrepresentative colonial government. Most inhabitants of African origin still had no vote. The 1938 riots were a protest against low wages and their colonial status.

Two Jamaicans of great stature rose to the fore in this difficult period. One was Alexander Bustamante, an important figure in the Trade Union movement, the other was Norman Washington Manley, the island's leading barrister. Cousins and rivals, these national heroes were instrumental in Jamaica's struggle for independence.

In 1944 the British admitted a new constitution based on universal adult suffrage, and the voting rolls swelled from 20,000 to more than 650,000. Full independence came on August 6, 1962.

Jamaica remains part of the British Commonwealth. There is a governor-general representing the Crown and a parliamentary system consisting of an appointed senate and an elected house of representatives. The main instrument of policy is the cabinet, headed by the prime minister.

Sugar continues to be a major source of wealth, but Jamaica is now one of the largest producers of bauxite in the world. Light industry has been encouraged and tourism ranks high as a source of foreign income.

Independence gave a new fillip to education and the arts. Theatre, painting, sculpture, dance and literature are all flourishing and the island's reggae music is sweeping the world. Jamaicans still go to the United States and Great Britain for an education, but more and more they see a future for themselves at home.

The blue sky looks down on sleek, modern offices of New Kingston.

Where to Go

Kingston
Pop. 750,000

Kingston is neither pretty nor charming. It is much what you would expect a Caribbean port city to be—crowded, bustling, sometimes aggressive, encompassing the lifestyles of the poor and the luxurious villas of the rich. You may not care to linger, but you cannot ignore it if you want to know what Jamaica is all about.

It was founded in the 17th century after most of the old capital, Port Royal, had slipped into the sea as the result of an earthquake (an act of God, some muttered darkly). In 1872 the seat of government was transferred here from Spanish Town. Much of Kingston was destroyed in the 1907 earthquake, then rebuilt in more solid materials.

The city itself falls into two sections—downtown or old Kingston, where some semblance of the original city plan is still evident, and uptown Kingston, where the ground rises towards the cooler, airy foothills of the Blue Mountains.

New Kingston
New Kingston is a modern development of hotels, banks, offices and shops within the uptown area. Some of the city's loveliest houses are near at hand, built in the colonial style, with wide verandahs and cut-out wooden decoration. Floors and ceilings are usually of prime Jamaican mahogany. The gardens are studded with massive tropical trees and clumps of riotous shrubs.

Devon House, to the east along Hope Road, is one of

the finest of these. Beautifully restored by the Jamaica National Trust, it stands in its own spacious grounds and is open to the public daily. The house has been refurbished in the styles of different periods in Jamaican history, and there are regular guided tours.

Built in 1881 by George Stiebel, one of the first black millionaires in the Caribbean, the house passed through the hands of other prominent Jamaican families. The government acquired it in 1964.

The former staff quarters have been turned into craft shops where you can buy basketry, carving, embroidery and stationery, and there is an "olde tyme" Jamaican bakery and two pleasant restaurants and a bar. You may wish to try the spine-chilling concoction known as a Devon Duppy.

Half-Way Tree is the name of a main intersection. No one knows what it was half-way between, but the tree in question was a huge cottonwood. Rain washed away the earth around the roots, forming a convenient resting place for market people coming down from the Blue Mountains with their produce.

An eastward jaunt along Hope and Old Hope Roads takes you to the **Hope Botanical Gardens,** the largest in the Caribbean. You may wish to hire a guide to help you find your way around the 200 acres of exotic plants. The greenhouses are worth a visit.

The **University of the West Indies** is nearby. It was founded in 1948 with only 33 students. Now there are thousands on the campus which is situated on the site of the old Mona and Papine sugar estates.

Downtown Kingston

Downtown Kingston is noisier and busier. There are certain sections you should keep out of, as they have nothing to offer a tourist in any case. But the waterfront has had a facelift. Its broad boulevards, skyscrapers, the showpiece Conference Centre, are sparkling new—and spotless, ever since littering started to carry heavy fines!

Jamaica's **National Gallery** is housed in the Roy West Building in the ocean-front area of the Kingston Mall. The collection comprises works by Albert Huie, Alvin Marriott and Edna Manley—all important names in Jamaican art. Edna Manley, sculptor of the beautiful and dignified *Negro Aroused* (1939), was the wife of the country's first prime minister, Norman Manley, and mother of another prime minister, Michael Manley. Also on display is a controversial statue of Bob Marley.

Other points of interest in downtown Kingston:

At the west end of Harbour Street is Kingston's **Craft Market,** taking up a big modern building. This is the spot to look for basketry, carving, embroidery and thousands of examples of straw weaving—not to mention animated conversation and good-natured bargaining.

Little water taxis leave from nearby Pier No. 2 on their way to historic Port Royal (see p. 24).

The **Institute of Jamaica** near Harbour Street houses the finest collection of books and papers on the West Indies. Among the documents preserved here are the Shark Papers. An American barque, the *Nancy,* happily engaged

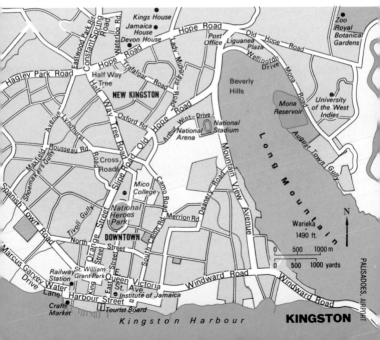

in illicit trading in 1799, was stopped by a British vessel. The American captain tossed the ship's log overboard and substituted a false one. Some miles away an officer fishing from another British ship hooked a shark. Cut open, it revealed the incriminating log which led to the conviction of the *Nancy*'s captain and owners.

The **St. William Grant Park**, once the centre of Kingston, is bounded by four streets, known as North, South, East and West Parade.

The **Ward Theatre** on North Parade is a showcase for productions of all kinds.

At Christmas it comes magnificently into its own with the magic of Kingston's celebrated Christmas pantomime. The stern brick building on East Parade is the Coke Chapel, dating from 1841.

Kingston Parish Church on South Parade warrants a visit. The original brick building, erected in 1699, was destroyed in the 1907 earthquake but the present structure still contains the black marble gravestone of Admiral Benbow, who died in 1702 after a battle with the French. There are also three wall monuments by John Bacon, a prominent 18th-century British sculptor.

Around Kingston

North-east of the capital lie the beautiful **Blue Mountains.** The best way to go is via PAPINE, GUAVA RIDGE and MAVIS BANK. In this area you'll see a number of small houses surrounded by vegetable gardens —the source of most of Kingston's produce. The road is not always good, especially after heavy rain. You should start early, take a sweater (the air is much cooler) and strong shoes. There are some delightful

Introducing Jamaica's Birds

There's an old Jamaican folksong about birds which says that "some of dem a-holla, some a-bawl". The klingkling does neither but has a piercing whistle. Jet-black, perfectly composed in human company, its real name is the Greater Antillean Grackle.

The turkey buzzard is known here as John Crow, supposedly after an unpopular parson whose bald head, scarlet with sunburn, rose on a startlingly long neck from his clerical garments.

The doctor bird, a swallow-tailed humming-bird with a green breast and black body, has a typically Jamaican sense of the dramatic, for it loves to show off in front of brilliantly coloured flowers. It's Jamaica's national bird.

walks in the area and a feeling of splendid isolation as pale mountain mists wreathe and part over plunging valleys and lush vegetation.

Mavis Bank is the starting-point for the climb, a tough, three-hour trek up to Blue Mountain Peak (7,402 feet). The classic hike involves starting out at 2 a.m., so that you arrive at the summit in time for a sensational sunrise. The more northerly road to NEWCASTLE and HARDWAR GAP brings you within range of Hollywell National Forest, an ideal spot for bird-watching.

Another recommended excursion from Kingston (19 miles to the north) is to **Castleton Gardens.** Founded in 1862, they cover 15 acres in the Wag Water Valley, stretching down to the fern-sprinkled banks of the river itself.

This is one of the most richly stocked gardens in the Caribbean, with a great variety of

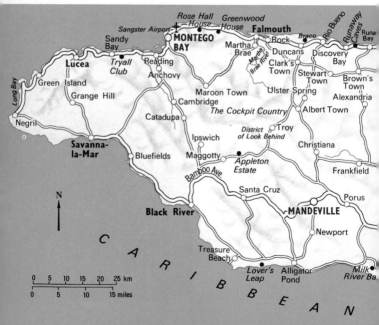

native and exotic plants, and it is worth hiring the services of a guide to show you around. Castleton registers over 100 inches of rain a year, so take suitable footwear, a swimsuit for bathing in the Wag Water River and possibly a picnic lunch so that you can make a day of it.

🛍 Port Royal

To get to Port Royal you can either take a water taxi from Pier No. 2 or drive there

on the Palisadoes road. The land route passes Long Mountain which sports a martello (watch) tower on its slopes and a fort at its foot (wedged against the Caribbean cement factory). Rock Fort was built in 1694 and rebuilt in 1792, forming with the tower part of the defence system against the French.

Port Royal was once the wickedest and most debauched city in the New World. Here the pirates caroused, rum and

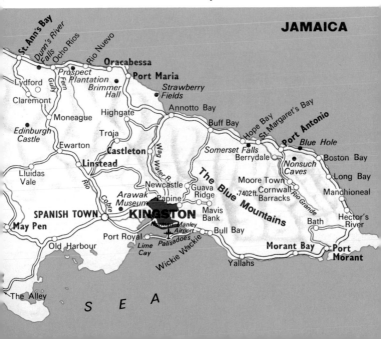

money flowed, pleasure was sweet and death often quick and violent.

In its heyday, Spanish gold and silver were the coinage of the town. Several thousand inhabitants erected buildings up to four storeys high. Cabinetmakers, wig makers and tailors set up shop. Gaming houses and brothels flourished. The rents were as high as in London, the fashions as elegant, the candelabra and plate just as fastidiously polished. There were several churches for the conscience-stricken, a prison and even a "house of correction for lazy strumpets".

And then, suddenly, on June 7, 1692, two-thirds of the town sank under the sea. Violent earthquakes claimed the lives of more than a thousand people, toppled the buildings, opened the land into gulping fissures and sent Port Royal to a watery and well-deserved end with the help of a tidal wave. Some people claim that on stormy days you can still hear the doleful tolling of submerged church bells.

Attempts to resuscitate the town were thwarted by fire in 1704, a disastrous succession of hurricanes and another earthquake in 1907. Long before this, it had relinquished any claim to importance and survives now as a quiet little backwater, placidly basking in the sun at the edge of Kingston Harbour.

If you approach by road, pay a visit to Morgan's Harbour, situated within the walls of the old naval dockyard. From there you can look over to the mournful salt marsh of Gallows Point where the last of the pirate hangings took place in 1831.

Within Port Royal itself, you will want to see **St. Peter's Church,** built in 1725 to replace the earlier churches which disappeared in the earthquake and the fire. The interior houses a brass hanging lamp and a superb organ loft of 18th-century Jamaican workmanship, as well as memorials to multitudes of young British naval officers who died of yellow fever, "the fever of the country" as it is described on the marble plaques.

A couple of dollars to the guide will also result in your viewing the communion plate. A silver tankard and some other objects are said to have belonged to that old reprobate, Henry Morgan himself, the British pirate turned patriot.

Outside the church you'll find the tomb of Louis Galdy, a Frenchman who was a refugee from religious persecution.

The famous earthquake resulted in his being swallowed into a yawning crack in the ground and thrown out again into the sea, where he swam to a boat and managed to save himself. He was later instrumental in having the church rebuilt.

The Police Training Depot contains both the remains of Fort Charles and a small maritime museum situated within the fort. They're open daily.

Fort Charles is the only one of the six original forts to have survived Port Royal's manifold disasters. Founded in 1656, it was named after Charles II of England. The prow-shaped fort once stood at the water's edge but land movements have shifted it to an inland position.

Henry Morgan was responsible for strengthening the construction, and Horatio Nelson spent a few weeks here as commander in 1779, keeping watch for the French invasion which never came. The guide will point out the area known as Nelson's Quarterdeck. He will also show you the so-called Giddy House, the old Royal Artillery Store, now tilted at a crazy angle.

The **Naval Hospital,** built in 1819 mainly for sufferers from yellow fever, has been renovated as a museum. On the ground floor is a department dedicated to the restoration of objects found in the harbour near Port Royal—candelabra, bottles, silver, bone and ivory articles. This is one of the richest 17th-century archaeological sites in the world and experts from all round the globe have helped with the work of salvage and restoration. Many of the recovered objects are displayed in the museum, along with objects from the excavations of Arawak Indian sites.

Spanish Town

The Spanish called it Villa de la Vega, "town on the plain". It was their capital for more than a hundred years. When the British took over, it remained the island's capital for another two centuries. In 1872 the seat of government was transferred to Kingston, and Spanish Town went into decline. The area of interest covers only one square mile, but a square mile full of charm and history.

If you drive there from Kingston, stop on the way at the **White Marl Arawak Museum,** about 10 miles from the city. Situated on an old Arawak site, it houses some of the most important Arawak Indian finds in the country. **27**

Spanish Town itself (pop. 40,000) is set on the banks of the River Cobre. The only thing Spanish about it now is its name, but the **Cathedral Church of St. James** stands on the site of a Spanish chapel demolished by Oliver Cromwell's soldiers. The church the British built was wrecked by a hurricane and replaced by the present, predominantly brick structure in 1714. Memorial plaques and tombs bear some familiar names in Jamaican history. The brick-and-wood steeple was added in 1831.

Once they had taken Spanish Town over, the British set to work to make it into a worthy capital for this, the most valuable of all Britain's West Indian possessions. For the centre of town, they designed a graceful little square. There stood the governor's residence, **King's House,** burnt out but reconstructed now to house a folk museum. On the north side of the square is a

John Bacon **memorial** to Admiral George Rodney, who saved Jamaica from French invasion in 1782. The cupola was an afterthought to protect the statue. The cannon came from the surrendering French flagship, *Ville de Paris.*

On the south side of the pocket park is the courthouse, built in the early 19th century. The beautifully colonnaded red-brick-and-wood structure, east, is the **House of Assembly,** erected in the 1760s, restored and altered several times since. In the surrounding streets are the remains of some fine old Georgian houses.

Worth noticing is the **Baptist Church** on the corner of William and French Streets. It is also known as Phillippo's church after the missionary, James Phillippo, who raised the money for the church which opened in 1827. The nearby 18th-century barracks also merit attention.

On your way back from Spanish Town to Kingston, you pass downstream of what is reputed to be the first cast-iron bridge in the Americas.

Monuments from colonial days give old-world look to Spanish Town, once Jamaica's capital.

Eastern Jamaica

You can approach the east coast of Jamaica from two different directions: north by way of Castleton (see p. 24) or by following the southern coast road through Morant Bay. (Exceptionally heavy summer rains may affect the latter route, so check with the Tourist Board before you set out.)

Along the southern route, PALM BEACH and WICKIE WACKIE have little to commend them except their names. At BULL BAY there is a turnoff to the mini-attraction of **Cane River Falls,** once the centre of an area held in terror by Three-Fingered Jack.

His real name was Jack Mansong and he was a runaway slave. When his attempt to lead a slave revolt failed, he took to the hills and sought the advice of an *obeah,* or magic man. Armed with the strongest magic possible, he turned to robbery and his name became infamous throughout the area. He lost two of his fingers in a struggle with a pursuer, and when he was finally killed, in 1781, his head and hand were carried to Kingston preserved in a bucket of rum, macabre but undeniable evidence for claiming the £300 reward set for his capture.

MORANT BAY, the next point of interest, was the scene of the 1865 uprising in which Paul Bogle, one of Jamaica's national heroes, tried to obtain justice for the liberated slaves (see p. 17). The courthouse, the focal point of the revolt, honours his memory with a statue by Edna Manley.

Just past Morant Bay is PORT MORANT, set in the middle of extensive coconut and banana groves. Here you turn off to **Bath** (about 7 miles away), which is noted for its mineral springs. Officially named the Mineral Bath of St. Thomas the Apostle, this spa was first developed in 1699. For a while it was a fashionable watering place. The very high radio-activity of the water still attracts sufferers from rheumatism and skin disease. There is a pleasant little hotel with an old-fashioned restaurant and spa facilities.

Bath also has a Botanical Garden. It is tiny and more like a town park than anything else but charming for this very reason. You can continue on the Bath road to the east coast. There, MANCHIONEAL, a small fishing village, is followed by the beautiful white sands of **Long Bay** and **Boston Bay.** Try some of the jerk pork on sale in this area. The meat is hotly peppered before being smoked in the open over a pimento-wood fire. The vendor will cut you off a slice on the try-before-you-buy principle. There may be roasted yams going, too. The cooking method originated with the Maroons (see p. 13). You can't quite claim to have visited Jamaica unless you have sampled jerk pork or its less authentic equivalent, jerk chicken.

Continuing up the coast past Marbella Club at DRAGON BAY with its luxury villas, you come to the **Blue Hole,** also known as the Blue Lagoon. It deserves every adjective that has ever been lavished upon it. Translucent water of the deepest ultramarine lies surrounded by dark green vegetation. Have a drink, water-ski, hire a glass-bottomed boat to explore the sea life or simply capture the memory of it all with your camera.

Pass on, while your energy lasts, to SAN SAN BEACH and indulge in a tour of the grounds of Frenchman's Cove, once reputedly the most expensive hotel in the world.

You can water-ski, swim or simply dream at the lovely Blue Lagoon.

Port Antonio

Refreshed by rain showers drifting over from the Blue Mountains, Port Antonio (pop. 10,000) is one of the greenest spots in Jamaica. It is a centre for the Jamaican banana trade and was an early mecca for tourism, celebrated before Montego Bay or Ocho Rios were ever heard of. They have since surpassed it in tourist numbers, but Port Antonio, in contrast, offers a feeling of exclusivity and calm. It's also noted for its deep-sea fishing, with marlin, wahoo, kingfish, bonefish, yellowfish and dolphin (a fighting fish, not the porpoise variety) running within half a mile of the shore.

Cradled by the bushy arms of the mountains, Port Antonio has two superb harbours, divided by the Titchfield peninsula. The town itself used to be called Titchfield after the English estate of the Duke of Portland. Fort George, on the tip of the peninsula, was built to protect the area. Its walls remain and can be visited but now they enclose the buildings of Titchfield School.

The two harbours, rather unimaginatively named East and West, are flanked by Navy Island, once owned by the film star Errol Flynn. His name and anecdotes of hard living—and harder playing— have entered into the area's history.

Folly Estate stands on the east side of East Harbour. Legend and fact have become incredibly confused, but the truth is that it was acquired at the beginning of the century by an American, Alfred Mitchell, who built a large concrete mansion there. Mitchell and his wife, a Tiffany from New York, lived periodically in Jamaica until he died in 1912. In 1938 the roof fell in as a result of the corrosion of the iron reinforcing rods. (The legend, far more entertaining than the facts, relates that he brought his bride to the house and it collapsed on their arrival.) Nowadays little is left except a story that gets better with the arrival of every tourist.

If you enjoy lookout points, it is well worth going up to **Bonnie View.**

The **Nonsuch Caves** offer an easy expedition 5 miles inland from Port Antonio. They are situated at the Seven Hills of Athenry, a working plantation of pimento trees, banana, coconut and citrus groves, formerly owned by the United Fruit Company. There is a view to the coast and a fine aspect of Blue Mountain Peak.

The caves once lay under water and preserve fossilized remains of ocean species. A guide takes you through the caves, which are well lit and have good paths.

There are two Maroon villages near Port Antonio—MOORE TOWN and CORNWALL BARRACKS. Maroons were runaway slaves (see p. 13) who based themselves in outback areas and harassed white settlements. All their townships have an administration peculiar to them, under the control of a colonel who presides over a village council or *osufu*. They look no different from any other Jamaican towns and there is no touristic reason to go there.

The mountains give rise to numerous streams and rivers and the most celebrated of them all is the **Rio Grande.** No, not that Rio Grande, but Jamaica's own lighthearted version. The planters who owned the great estates used to use bamboo rafts for transporting produce and for the Sunday afternoon amusement of their friends and family. Errol Flynn tried such a trip, liked it and popularized it. Now rafting on the Rio Grande is one of *the* things to do in Jamaica and it lives up to its reputation.

The rafts are constructed of long bamboo rods with a seat built at the stern for two people. The barefoot and highly experienced raftsman poles from the front. The whole trip lasts two and a half hours. The starting point is BERRYDALE and you step ashore at RAFTERS' REST, St. Margaret's Bay. A man will drive your car from Berrydale to the spot at which you disembark. Group transport can also be arranged through your hotel.

Every trip turns out to be an individual experience as you float through calm water between shingle banks, manœuvre through rushing (but safe and shallow) rapids and pass under the overhanging branches of tropical trees. There is time to sun, or to picnic and bathe along the bank. For the romantically inclined, a night trip is indicated, available during full moon. The Tunnel of Love bears Errol Flynn's personal recommendation.

West of St. Margaret's Bay, near HOPE BAY, are the **Somerset Falls** where the Daniels River plunges through a series of cascades and pools to the sea.

After Hope Bay the road passes through BUFF BAY to the township of ANNOTTO. A sleepy enough place all week,

The good life is an everyday matter in North Coast resorts.

The North Coast

Ocho Rios

The area of Ocho Rios, extending some 60 miles from Annotto to Discovery Bay, is one of Jamaica's great tourist successes. Here, and at Montego Bay, you can buy and

it comes alive on Saturdays when the market takes over with its colourful display of mangoes, bananas, paw-paw, ackee, soursop and piles of other fruit and vegetables.

promenade in your most glamourous resort wear—in the evening long skirts for women and tropical suits for men and an elegant minimum during the day. Not that Jamaica goes too far in this direction, but Caribbean shopping is one of the attractions of the northern area and it's nice to be able to show off your purchases.

The name Ocho Rios may have come from the Spanish meaning "eight rivers"—which would be an exaggerated assessment of the number of significant waterways. It is more likely to be a corruption of *las chorreras* ("spouts") referring to the waterfalls in the area.

This part of the northern coastline is important in New World history with the name of Christopher Columbus figuring prominently. Proceeding westward along the coast you pass through PORT MARIA, main town of the parish of St. Mary, with some beautiful views over the coastline. The seaside brick church at the eastern end of the harbour was built in about 1830 by a Scottish planter, Archibald Stirling, for his slaves.

Inland from Port Maria is **Brimmer Hall,** a famous great house set on a working plantation. You can explore the estate on a "jitney", an open buggy pulled by a tractor—a gentle enough excursion but wear casual clothes and remember to take a hat. Tours around the plantation leave several times a day, every day of the week.

With their quick sense of humour and their colourful, poetic approach to the English language, Jamaicans make great guides. You are bound to enjoy their explanations of the life cycle of a banana plant, how to climb a coconut palm or carry a bunch of bananas on your head. Enjoy coconut water fresh from the nut, with or without rum. You cannot visit the house, but there are shops, refreshments and a swimming pool.

ORACABESSA, a little banana port, gained fame because of the two celebrated British writers who lived in the area. Ian Fleming was married in the registry office in Port Maria; Noël Coward was a witness and tied the good-luck shoe to the back of his own car by mistake. One of Fleming's best-known tales, *Dr. No,* was filmed in Jamaica, part of it in the bauxite factory at Ocho Rios.

You can visit Noël Coward's home, **Firefly,** built on a beautiful headland overlooking the sea. Two baby grands occupy **35** the small drawing-room, and many of the playwright's mementoes, scores, programmes and scripts as well as his paintings of Jamaican scenery are stacked about.

RIO NUEVO, westward along the coast, is the site of the battle of the same name where in 1658 Ysassi, the Spanish titular governor, was defeated by the British under E. D'Oyley.

Just past COUPLES a road turns off to **Prospect Plantation,** a property specializing in beef and in lime trees, but with a full complement of all tropical produce from bananas to cassava. You can take a "jitney" tour similar to the one available at Brimmer Hall (see p. 35) or do your sightseeing on horseback. Three trails are marked, all of them delightful. An experienced guide accompanies you. You should reserve a day in advance.

There's a wealth of activities available in the Ocho Rios area, with scuba, deep-sea fishing, horse-back riding, polo at Drax Hall and nearby Chukka Cove, golf, shopping at Pineapple Place, Coconut Grove or Ocean Village, or simply swimming and sunning. But your holiday would not be complete without a few excursions into the back country.

The **Carñosa Gardens** cover 20 acres with 14 waterfalls, a restaurant, lily ponds and an aviary among other attractions.

Just past the village of Ocho Rios, a turn inland from TURTLE BEACH takes you to **Shaw Park Gardens,** worth at least a couple of hours for unhurried enjoyment of the landscaped park and tropical blooms.

Further on, **Fern Gully,** an old riverbed now converted

into a road, meanders some 700 feet up through shadowy trees, lianas and hardwoods. Unfortunately, car fumes have had their effect on the ferns and there are fewer now than there used to be. Near LYDFORD are the Reynold's bauxite mines.

Following the road on to MONEAGUE, you pass by the site of a disappearing lake which seems to have its origin underground. In 1810 it covered hundreds of acres and flooded out a sugar factory, but by 1900 it had vanished. Legend says that once the lake rises it stays high until it has claimed a life by drowning.

West of Moneague are the remains of **Edinburgh Castle,** built in 1763 by a red-haired Scotsman, Lewis Hutchinson. He developed the rather unusual hobby of shooting down everyone who passed along the

Luxury accommodation a few steps from the beach at Ocho Rios.

lonely road from peepholes in his castle and then throwing the decapitated bodies into a pit. He was tried and sentenced to be hanged. Totally unrepentant, he left £100 at the foot of the scaffold for a monument to be erected to his memory. He even composed the epitaph. It was never used.

Back along the coast, west of Reynold's bauxite pier, you come to **Dunn's River Falls,** the loveliest spot in the area. The water cascades over rock terraces and through pools to the sea. You needn't be very adventurous to climb the falls, assisted by experienced guides. Of course, you wear a swim-suit for the occasion and get doused with cold water, but it's all very easy and pleasant. Your hotel will also have details about the Dunn's River Feast, held weekly. Dancing, music and swimming if you feel like it and a Jamaican "feast". The fun begins in the early evening and continues for as long as you do.

ST. ANN'S BAY is the capital of the parish of the same name. Its most famous son was one of the great black leaders of this century, Marcus Garvey. SEVILLE, to the west, is the site of the earliest Spanish settlement in Jamaica, founded in 1510 near the spot where

Columbus first anchored (see p. 12). Under the Spanish the town was known as Sevilla Nueva. The bronze Columbus monument, erected in 1957, was cast in the explorer's native city of Genoa. The church behind the statue contains stones from the original Spanish church, which stood off to the west.

More hotels edge the blue water just before RUNAWAY BAY, said to be the spot from which the last Spanish governor, Ysassi, embarked for Cuba after his resounding defeat by the British. (However, modern historians tend to think he sailed from Port Maria.) Then again the bay may have acquired its name because it was a departure point for runaway slaves. In any case, tradition firmly associates Ysassi's name with **Runaway Caves** and claims that he hid here before making good his escape. These limestone caves, first used by the Arawak Indians, later became the haunt of pirates and smugglers and a place of refuge for slaves. They were rediscovered in 1838, and 7 miles of passageway have been explored to date.

The **Green Grotto,** 120 feet underground, is a vaulted chamber filled with eerie water. Your guide will take you for a trip around it in a metal boat. This underground tidal lake, part salt-, part fresh-water, is populated by crayfish, mullet and eel—all blind.

The memory of Columbus is ever-present on this part of the coast and DISCOVERY BAY, with PUERTO SECO at the eastern entry to it, is where the great man supposedly landed for the first time. Puerto Seco means "dry harbour" since he found no fresh water around. There is a public beach here with a water-play area for children, a favourite picnic spot for locals.

Further along on the cliff road to Montego Bay, Columbus Park features relics of early Jamaican history including a water wheel and huge sugar cauldrons.

RIO BUENO, on the boundary of the parishes of St. Ann and Trelawny, likewise claims a Columbus landing (the man was tireless). This time he found water. And all along the coast are more silvery beaches, such as BRACO and TRELAWNY, and more turquoise sea.

Water fun at Dunn's River Falls —just the thing for a hot day.

Montego Bay
Pop. 125,000

Jamaica's second largest city, Montego Bay supposedly got its name from the Spanish word *manteca* (lard). Passing ships took on supplies of pork and beef fat from this coastal point, and some early documents even refer to it as Lard Bay.

Mo' Bay (as you are soon likely to call it) entered the touristic scene early in the century when a certain Dr. Mc-Catty, advanced for his time, advocated the bracing virtues of salt-water bathing. He and his friends formed the Doctor's Beach Club. This was in 1906. Nobody doubts the virtues (or pleasures) of sea-bathing any more and Montego Bay has gone into Caribbean history. Sugar and bananas take second place to the tourist industry, but a good part of the international set has now moved on.

Montego Bay falls naturally into three areas—the coastal strip, with hotels and shopping plazas, the hills behind and the urban district.

Centrally situated in the city centre, the **Cage** dates from 1807 and used to be a gaol for runaway slaves. The late 18th-century parish church of St. James, rebuilt after the 1957 earthquake, contains two monuments by John Bacon, the British sculptor responsible for the Rodney memorial in Spanish Town.

The St. James' **Craft Market** at the bottom of Market Street is an open-air spot for baskets, carving, embroidery and straw goods. You'll find duty-free shops scattered about Montego Bay, but the big concentration is at the Freeport, on a small peninsula west of the city.

Fort Montego, opposite Walter Fletcher Beach, was built in the mid-18th century, but never needed to be used. Pay a visit to Richmond Hill for a view over Montego Bay. It is equally pleasant at night and there is a good restaurant.

The Montego Bay area stretches 26 miles east to the **Martha Brae,** one of Jamaica's rafting rivers. The experience is similar to the Rio Grande (see p. 32) but this waterway is more winding and the trip takes an hour and a quarter. You start at RAFTERS' VILLAGE where there are picnic

Learn to sail, listen to calypso. Both have the same easy rhythm.

Drifting down the Martha Brae, the lazy way to see the country.

grounds, gifts shops, refreshments and a bar. Feathery bamboo fringes the river as you drift through banana plantations, fields of sugar cane and yam. Birds a plenty—small green parakeets, woodpeckers and the energetic bananaquit—serenade you on your way. The trip ends at ROCK. Afterwards a bus takes you back to the starting point.

A mile to the west, **Falmouth** boasts an admirable concentration of Georgian buildings. Market Street was

Water Square is the Court House, reconstructed in Palladian style after being gutted by fire in 1926.

The capital of Trelawny parish was moved from Martha Brae to Falmouth when the river mouth silted up. Sugar and rum made the town prosperous. It was named after the Falmouth in Cornwall, birthplace of Governor William Trelawny.

There are several estates which can be visited in the

used as background scenery for the movie version of *Papillon*. The Methodist manse at the bottom of the street was built in 1799 by the Barretts, the family of poetess Elizabeth Barrett Browning. Now sadly decayed, the house was once an elegant example of the architecture of its time. Near

The White Witch

A 19th-century mistress of Rose Hall gave the great house such an ominous reputation that for years it was considered too spooky to live in.

Annie Palmer arrived at the estate in 1820 as a beautiful but restless young bride. Mixtures of fact, rumour and superstition would have us believe that she poisoned her first husband, strangled her second, and stabbed No. 3. Along the way she allegedly assassinated the odd lover, as well as terrifying the local slaves with her white black-magic. She was only 29 when they buried her in the grounds of Rose Hall; the "white witch" had been strangled by an unknown hand.

43

area. **Greenwood House** dates from the early 19th century and used to be owned by a member of the Barrett family. It is beautifully furnished and

The market brings exotic fruit and vegetables and bustling activity to the streets of Falmouth.

contains a collection of early musical instruments as well as one or two well-authenticated "duppies".

Rose Hall, restored from a ruin at great expense, was the home of the infamous "white witch". Built in 1760, this was always one of the finest houses in Jamaica, with its mahogany

panelling, precious fruitwood and superb staircase.

Inland from Montego Bay, near ANCHOVY, you can observe and photograph rare birds at Lisa Salmon's **Bird Sanctuary,** also known as Rocklands Feeding Station. The humming-birds fly down to drink from hand-held bottles; feeding takes place in the late afternoon. Children under five are not admitted.

Western Jamaica

The west coast of the island, especially the area around Negril, is Jamaica's most recent tourist phenomenon.

Starting from Montego Bay, you pass TRYALL, where there is an old water-wheel marking the site of a sugar factory, now disappeared. LUCEA, with its pretty harbour, used to be a busy sugar port. Up on a hill, Fort Charlotte can be visited. **Negril** got its name in the 15th century from the Spanish, who called the place Negrillo. In 1720, the infamous pirate "Calico Jack" Rackham was captured here. Among his crew were two particularly fierce fighters, who turned out to be women—and pregnant women at that. They were about the only ones to escape the gallows.

Far from trying to emulate Montego Bay, Negril cultivates an away-from-it-all image. In the days when there were hippies, this is where they headed, leading the easy life in tents and huts along the beautiful 7-mile beach. Negril has come a long way since then but the emphasis is still on casual living. You can rent charming, Jamaican-style thatched huts with waterbeds or hammocks, eat plenty of native and natural food and take off more with fewer eyebrows raised.

Negril Harbour or Bloody Bay, a crescent loop of sand, is more appealing than its name, which dates back to whaling days. **Long Bay** turns out to be miles of shimmering sand, barely rolling down to a sea as warm as any you'll find off Jamaican coasts.

Life is most light-hearted at the west end, between South Negril River and the lighthouse. Here the coast is rocky, with deep inlets for swimming and snorkelling. The sunsets from this far-westerly point are technicolour displays of violet, orange and saffron. Try to catch one of the exhibitions of cliff diving.

The easiest way to see the other-worldly landscape of the

Cockpit Country is on a day excursion on the Governor's Coach, the tourist train from Montego Bay. This strange potholed countryside, carved out of limestone, has thick vegetation and sharp peaks. The fugitive slaves hid out here from the British (see p. 13), and their descendants still live in the area in Maroon villages.

The train tour (complete with a calypso band to keep you on your toes) crosses a variety of landscapes, offering a kaleidoscopic view, however brief, of the "real" Jamaica. One stop is at the little town of CATADUPA, positively ablaze with lengths of coloured cotton and synthetic fabric. There, friendly seamstresses will measure you in a whisk and have a finished shirt or dress waiting for you on your way back. The excursion also includes a visit to Ipswich Cave and the slightly more riotous exploration of the Appleton rum factory near MAGGOTTY.

Mandeville

Mandeville, 65 miles west of Kingston, is the place to retreat when you feel like resting in a cool, calm atmosphere. Once it was very popular among the British, who took refuge there when the weather was too hot or sticky in Kingston. For it is a hill town, set 2,000 feet above sea-level with temperatures ranging from 55° to 85°F. It is accessible by road from all parts of the island and planes fly in from Kingston and Mo' Bay. Bauxite is the source of its present wealth. A nearby alumina plant has spawned a large American colony. The town still has an English flavour, emphasized by the imposing Georgian courthouse, the stone church and the oldest golf-links on the island, Manchester Club.

From Mandeville, you can make outings west along beautiful **Bamboo Avenue**, where the trees form a canopy over your head, or south-west to **Lover's Leap**, a sheer cliff plunging down 1,500 feet to the sea. It's a relatively short distance from Lover's Leap to the biscuit-coloured sands of **Treasure Beach.**

Heading back east along the coast, you can stop off at **Milk River Bath,** Jamaica's largest spa and the world's most radioactive. Water temperature is 92°F. A story (also attributed to the St. Thomas Spring at Bath) says the curative properties were discovered by a runaway slave whose wounds miraculously healed after bathing in the water.

There's room to spare on the 7-mile stretch of Negril beach, Jamaica's most relaxed resort. **47**

What to Do

Sports

The nice thing about an island is the ease with which you can get off it and into the water. The sea is never far away. It's calm, it's warm and the beaches are well set-up. Jamaica is also the place to get your tennis up to scratch—or your golf.

Water Sports

Swimming. Many hotels have their own private beach—though there are plenty of public ones, too—and larger hotels offer freshwater pools. Bathing areas and pools are safety-patrolled from about 9 a.m. to 6 p.m. (the exact hours are usually indicated).

The best beaches are along the northern coast. The longest with the warmest water is at Negril, 7 miles of gently sloping white sand descending to a sea as welcoming as bathwater. For **surfing,** head east of Port Antonio to the breakers of Boston Bay.

Snorkelling. Chances are you won't even have to get wet to glimpse the colourful, tropical fish which are likely to be swimming at the end of every pier. However, for closer inspection you can hire equipment at hotels along the north coast, where the snorkelling is good almost anywhere. Runaway Bay is especially recommended. Other interesting spots include Kingston Bay and the pretty island of Lime Cay, accessible from Morgan's Harbour.

Reefs often lie within 100 yards of the shore. The water is clear and marine life is abundant with 50 varieties of coral, diverse varieties of sponge, sea urchins, starfish, worms and such fish as moonshine snapper, peacock flounders, french angels, small octopus, batfish and tangs. Guided snorkelling trips are available, and some hotels have instructors. There are also local diving centres which will help you improve your floating, resting and boat-entry techniques.

Boating. Most beach hotels have small sailing boats (Sunfish or Sailfish) for hire. Windsurfing is growing in popularity and instruction is available. For chartering a larger boat contact the Royal Jamaica Yacht Club in Port Royal. River rafting, a unique Jamaican experience, can be done on the Rio Grande, the Great River and the Martha Brae.

Fishing. Jamaica has fresh- and saltwater fish aplenty, in-

Daredevil diving from the rocks is not recommended for amateurs.

cluding the really big ones that run off Port Antonio. There is an annual International Fishing Tournament at Port Antonio in the autumn, one of the major deep-sea fishing spots in the Caribbean. There are also other tournaments in Port Antonio and an annual contest in Ocho Rios.

Mo's Bay is also a good centre. Among the fish you are likely to land are sailfish, blue marlin, wahoo, dolphin (the fighting fish), tuna, bonito, kingfish and barracuda. Marlin is the prize catch.

Spearfishing is generally permitted along the reefs (inquire locally) and you will find snapper, including red snapper, kingfish, mackerel and grouper. Coral is protected and must not be removed.

49

Fly-fishing, in many streams and rivers, may land Jamaican bass and mullet.

Sports Ashore

Tennis. Jamaica has an ample supply of courts and first-class players. Nearly all north-coast courts are free to hotel guests. Some hotels have a professional coach. If you are a serious player, inquire at the Jamaica Tourist Board about tennis package holidays.

Golf. Jamaica offers some excellent, and famous, courses. The best are clustered around Montego Bay. Beautifully laid out and never overcrowded, they include Tryall, Half Moon, Wyndham and Ironshore. Near Ocho Rios are the Upton and Runaway Bay. Visitors to Kingston have a choice of Constant Spring Golf Club and Caymanas Country Club. Mandeville has the 9-hole Manchester Golf Club.

Walking. Most enjoyable in the country with its thick vegetation, animated bird life and cooler temperatures. For information on mountain huts, walking trails or taking on Blue Mountain Peak (not for novices), contact the Jamaica Tourist Board.

Jogging. The world-wide keep-fit craze is well provided for and there is even a jogging

trail in uptown Kingston (at the Pegasus Hotel). Elsewhere, you will find trails at Ocho Rios (1 mile), at Montego Free Port (3 miles) and at Negril (about 4 miles), all laid out near the beach.

Horseback riding. Riding is particularly pleasant in the cool, hilly area near Mandeville, which has a riding school. There are also stables along the north coast. Inquire at your hotel for particulars. In Kingston, contact the Cay-

manas Golf and Country Club.

Spectator Sports. The British bequeathed cricket and matches are played from January to the end of August. You can watch soccer in the autumn and winter, and polo throughout the year at Caymanas Park in Kingston and Drax Hall near Ocho Rios. There is horse-racing at Caymanas Race Course, Kingston. Local newspapers give all the details.

Shopping

There are two categories of shopping in Jamaica—local goods, such as arts and crafts, and imported duty-free articles. You'll find clusters of shops of both kinds in the tourist areas. The main markets are the Kingston Straw or Craft Market by Harbour

The British introduced cricket, now Jamaica boasts some of the finest players in the world.

Street, the St. James' Market in Montego Bay and the markets in Ocho Rios and Porto Antonio.

Where the imports are concerned, it's helpful to have a good idea of what things cost back home. In that way you can judge how much you save on articles like Scottish cashmeres, French perfumes, Swiss watches, Japanese cameras, liquor and so on. You can take along anything you purchase except the "consumables", i.e. alcohol and tobacco. These are delivered to your exit port (or airport) on departure from the country. The system is reliable.

Take proof of your visitor's status with you when you go duty-free shopping. Payment is in Jamaican dollars, the only legal tender on the island.

As for local products, craft shops and markets sell carvings, straw goods, embroidered linen articles, shell work and hand-crafted jewellery. Prices—not the cheapest in the Caribbean—are likely to be higher in small boutiques (where you are not really expected to bargain) than in markets or at roadside stalls (where you bargain for all you're worth).

Rastafarian carving is often of a high standard. Look especially for objects in *lignum vitae*, a beautiful but very heavy rosy hardwood. The Rastafarians also produce woven belts and berets in the "Rasta" colours of red, gold, black and green. Black coral, hand cut and polished, and Jamaican gemstones are made into attractive jewellery. Fash-

calypso or reggae are another good souvenir; so are reproductions of old Jamaican maps and prints. Bookshops offer a wide selection of publications about the country.

For the gourmet back home, consider some Blue Mountain coffee beans or island spices, and a local bottle—of rum, Tia

ionable resort wear is available for men and women. It is well-cut and flattering, and has an unmistakable "Caribbean" look.

Scents and lotions from tropical flowers or based on lime or bay rum make attractive gifts. Records or cassettes of Jamaican music featuring

The flowers are to enjoy now, along with the smile. There are other souvenirs to carry home.

Maria liqueur, ready-mixed piña colada (rum, pineapple juice and coconut) or planter's punch cocktail—is usually welcome.

53

Nightlife

Most of the hotels have resident bands and offer floor shows every night. Calypso and reggae—an offshoot of rhythm and blues coloured by ska—add a lively beat, and everywhere you'll find a selection of discotheques. Once things get going people mix well. On the whole, you don't have to dress up, although with-it resort gear is part of the fun.

At beach and river parties, the entertainment and the food are usually superb. This is where you'll hear steel bands, watch limbo dancing and then shuffle all night to the reggae sound.

Most cinemas show films in English. Any opportunity to see Jamaican theatre should be

As famous as the music born from the Rastafarian movement, reggae, is the National Dance Theatre.

taken, especially if the National Dance Theatre is playing. The *patois* dialogue may make some of the plays difficult, even for English-speaking visitors, but the high standard of the performances, particu-

Rastas and Reggae

Jamaica's Rastafarian movement, often misunderstood, is a powerful cultural force, a religion and a search for national identity.

Rasta men grow their hair into "dreadlocks". The women wear long skirts and cover their heads. Rastafarians paint their houses with symbols of peace and love, and often display pictures of Ethiopia's Haile Selassie, viewed as an incarnation of God. Rastafarians are likely to be vegetarians and to smoke *ganja* (marijuana) as part of their religious experience. Some criminals have used this essentially peaceful movement as a cover for their activities.

On the positive side, an offshoot of the movement is reggae music. It developed from rhythm and blues, via the arm-swinging beat of ska. Singer Bob Marley made it popular far beyond Jamaica. Reggae fans abroad may be surprised to learn that the lyrics often contain a Rastafarian message.

larly surprising because theatre is amateur in Jamaica, more than makes up for any moments of incomprehension. The Jamaican Pantomime in the Ward Theatre, Kingston, is an absolute must if you're there between December 26 and April (but take a taxi home afterwards.)

A word of warning for more adventurous night owls. Treat red light districts with caution. The biggest and roughest are in Kingston and Montego Bay. **55**

Eating Out in Jamaica

If you prefer international cuisine, there's no problem. You will find all your favourite dishes from breakfast pancakes with syrup or bacon and eggs to roast beef and turkey.

If you're a health-food fan, you can relax in the knowledge that Jamaica is alert to vegetarianism. You will be well catered for, especially around Negril.

But it would be a great pity to miss out on the "real" cooking of the country. Jamaica has benefited from the culinary traditions of Africa, England and America, with each being adjusted to take into account the native produce. Food tends to be spicy. This stems from the country's early isolation, when many products had to be dried, pickled or salted for shipping to the island and spices were added in the cooking to spark up or disguise the flavour.

A Jamaican buffet, rightly called a "feast", is presented at least once a week by the main hotels. Otherwise you can order Jamaican food from the menu or sample the fare in local restaurants.

Starters

You may wish to try one of the **soups** such as pepperpot, containing callaloo (a type of spinach), okras and coconut milk. Pumpkin soup is good, too, as is conch. Conch (pronounced conk) is a large shellfish which can be very tough but comes into its own in fritters.

Stuffed crabs are delicately flavoured and spicy. You're also likely to find Solomon Gundy, a well-seasoned pickled herring, and patties, meat-filled pastry, as hors d'œuvres. Patties, Jamaica's staple snack, turn up everywhere from tea parties to street corner stalls. "Stamp and go", fish fritters, are often served with johnny cakes, a kind of deep-fried scone.

Seafood

All sorts of fresh **fish** appear on menus—kingfish (usually served in steaks), various kinds of snapper with red snapper the most highly rated, bonito and jack. Crayfish (spiny lobster) are fairly abundant—at a price.

Jamaica's national dish is salt fish and ackee but neither was originally indigenous to the country. The fish used to be imported as a cheap protein food for slaves and the ackee was brought to the island by Captain Bligh of *Bounty* fame. This rosy fruit is poisonous until it ripens and bursts open of its own accord, revealing a delicate yellow interior. Once cooked, ackee is rather like scrambled eggs (and usually offered as a breakfast dish) and it is excellent.

"Run dun" (also known as run-down fish) is made with shad or mackerel, gently simmered in boiled-down coco-

Jerk pork, cooked over pimento wood, is an east coast speciality.

nut milk. You'll find fry fish and bammie, a thick pancake made from cassava (manioc) flour, as a roadside snack or in small local restaurants. It's a speciality of the parish of St. Elizabeth, as are pepper shrimps.

Escovitched is made from any large fish, such as jack, cut into slices, sautéed then marinated in a peppery onion sauce containing vinegar.

Meat

Despise not the humble goat which seems to have more than its fair share of bones but can be very good curried and served with rice and green bananas. Pigeon is sometimes available and chicken is treated in a variety of ways. Jerk chicken consists of pieces smoked over pimento wood. Even more famous is **jerk pork,** a speciality of the parish of Portland and particularly associated with the area around Boston Beach. The recipe originated with the Maroons, who hunted wild boar and cooked it in this way. Jerk pork turns up at buffets but if ordering at a pork "pit" (the roadside stand), make sure you are given the proportion of lean and fat meat you want and ask for a sample slice **58** first.

Vegetables

In addition to the good old common **potato,** as popular here as elsewhere, in Jamaica you'll be served sweet potatoes, perfect with curry dishes; chocho, the prickly fruit of an aggressive vine with a mild, watery taste something like marrow; breadfruit, served boiled, fried or roasted and offering an unobtrusive starchy flavour; and yam, which is similar, a perfectly acceptable, bland carbohydrate. Green bananas are served boiled as a vegetable, while plantain, their larger, coarser cousin, is usually cut into slices, pressed and fried. **Rice 'n peas** (red beans) is a combination which turns up so often on the table it has been dubbed "the Jamaican coat-of-arms".

Desserts

Tarts and custards with coconut flavouring abound. Keep an eye out for the concoction known as matrimony, made of orange and star apples pulped and mixed with cream. Guava cheese is like a West Indian Turkish delight, sweet and chewy, and is made from guavas boiled down with sugar to form a jelly. Sweet potato pudding, English in approach, may be a little heavy for some tastes, but a few tablespoonfuls

of rum will send it on its way. Ripe **bananas** turn up in a variety of disguises, grilled, in fritters or in custards. A sprinkle of rum works wonders on many banana desserts, too. Banana bread, usually served at breakfast, is delicious.

Fruit

Here you come face to face with exotic, bewildering variety. Of course there will be oranges, mangoes (the best and least fibrous kinds are the Julie, Bombay and No. 11), papaya *(paw paw)*, served for breakfast or dessert with a squeeze of lime but very good, too, with a scoop of ice-cream.

You will also come across the sweetsop and soursop, rough-skinned fruits which can be eaten raw but are especially palatable turned into a milky drink. They are supposed to have aphrodisiac qualities. Sugar-cane lengths are sold along the road. Ask to have the cane stripped. Afterwards you chew on the stringy interior.

Beverages

All those fruits go into the blender to produce delicious alcoholic or non-alcoholic drinks. Coconut water is a roadside refresher. The green fruit is beheaded with a clean **59** sweep of a machete and you drink straight from the nut. Afterwards you pass the coconut back to the vendor who cuts off a coconut husk "spoon" so you can scrape out the jelly inside.

Red Stripe beer, the local lager, is strong and good. Most famous, of course, is the rum —light, aromatic, drunk in a variety of mixes but especially popular in a classic rum (or planter's) punch containing lime juice, sugar syrup and crushed ice and sometimes a sprinkle of nutmeg.

Imported wines are available but expensive. However Jamaica makes a pleasant wine from imported pulp.

Afterwards, to round it all off, there is Rumona, a rum-based liqueur, or delicious Tia Maria made from Blue Mountain coffee beans. Blue Mountain coffee itself is strong but excellent, one of the most prized coffees in the world, often blended with other varieties to give them character.

If, by any chance, you are offered mushroom tea, think twice. It is made from wild, psilocybin mushrooms and these, whether smoked, eaten raw or brewed into a tea, bring on hallucinations like those induced by LSD. It can be dangerous.

Excursions

Haiti

Haiti means "high country" in the language of the Arawak Indians who inhabited it. The name fits. Four-fifths of the land is mountainous, with peaks rising to 8,800 feet, sometimes dropping straight off to the sea.

From the air the country seems to be wrapped in a haze of greenish blue, softly clothing knobbed mountains and plunging valleys. On the ground, it resembles a sea of multi-coloured confetti, constantly stirred up, constantly changing. The people, in their gaiety, their welcome, their gentle courtesy and hospitality, have a kind of innocence as well as an untouchable dignity. It's not surprising that the theme of a lost Eden often appears in the work of Haitian artists.

Haiti occupies the western part of Hispaniola (the Dominican Republic takes up the other two-thirds of the island). It can claim to be the first black republic in the world— and was in fact, the only one for 150 years. But it's also the poorest and most densely populated country in the western

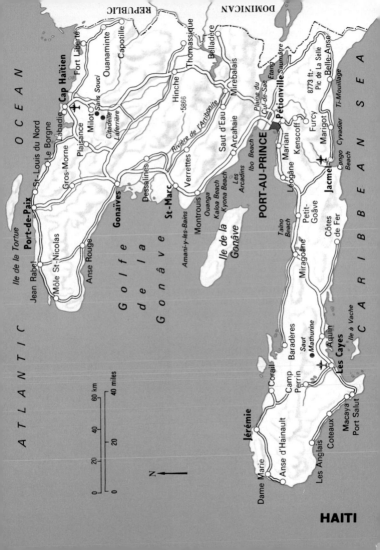

hemisphere, with something between 8 and 9 million people. Their language is Creole, an offshoot of French with various West African tongues, Spanish and English mixed in. Even French speakers need some time to adjust.

Here, conventional ideas about living standards lose their meaning and the word "civilized" takes on a wider meaning. Bare-footed peasant women walking down from the hills with baskets of vegetables on their heads have the demeanour of queens. The little boys, who cluster around and offer to show you the sights for a few gourdes (the local monetary unit), will do so honestly, faithfully and reliably. Their desire to learn something, as their ragged clothes, are not put on.

In Haiti, they bury the dead under heavy tombstones to keep them from returning to haunt the living. Nightly voodoo drums throb in the hills. But on Sundays, the same people who beat the drums will be in reverent attendance at church. At times Haiti seems like a dream.

This is not the usual sort of Caribbean holiday spot. No clichés can encompass it. There are beaches, some very good, some undeveloped or inaccessible except by jeep. There are the twin wonders of the Citadelle, built in the early 19th century to protect the country from French attack, and the grandiose ruins of Sans Souci palace. There is art blooming everywhere—in galleries, along the walls of buildings, spread on the sidewalks.

You can eat extraordinarily well and enjoy some of the wittiest and most charming company you are likely to run into anywhere. There is luxury, too, in the calm of Pétionville villas and hotels. On the other hand, you will see signs of poverty that may make you feel very uncomfortable.

Dark Haitian sails stand out against the dawning day. Boats carry produce to outlying islands and return home with a catch of fish for the market.

The Haitians themselves say that a visit to their country is a cultural experience in the widest sense of the term. Haiti may disturb you, move you or fascinate you. It is practically certain it will not leave you indifferent.

A Brief History

Columbus discovered the island on December 5, 1492, and named it Española or Hispaniola, "Spanish island". The resident Arawak Indians greeted the newcomers with their usual good nature, courtesy and gifts of gold trinkets. There may have been as many as a million Arawaks in 1492, but most of them were slaughtered or died off over the next 50 years. Then began the importation of slaves from West Africa, many from the coast of Guinea.

French Rule

About 1625, French and English buccaneers set up headquarters on Tortuga Island. The French corsairs gradually extended their interests to Haiti and created the settlement of Cap-Français (now Cap Haitien). Spain formally relinquished the western third of the island to France under the Treaty of Ryswick (1697).

This area, known as Saint-Domingue, became the richest of France's Caribbean colonies. Its profitable export trade included sugar, coffee, indigo, cacao and cotton. The French lived a life of luxury at the expense of the slaves. Ultimately, two factors precipitated the slaves' drive for freedom: news of the French Revolution and the unifying force of voodoo.

In 1791, half a million slaves revolted, set fire to estates and murdered plantation owners. Two years of disorder ended in 1793 with a proclamation of freedom for slaves. But the English and Spanish, taking advantage of the unsettled state of affairs began moving into the French possession; out of desperation, the French called on an ex-slave, a man of about 50 by the name of Toussaint l'Ouverture.

Toussaint succeeded in ousting both the Spanish and English, became Commander in Chief of the Saint-Domingue army and eventually, in 1801, governor of the country. Enlightened and far-sighted, he treated Europeans with fairness, welcoming them back as administrators, building up a strong army and attempting to restore the country's lost prosperity.

It was all too much for

Spectral and beautiful, King Henri-Christophe's palace of Sans Souci lies in ruins and nothing remains of the once splendid interior.

Napoleon, then the first consul of France. Not only did he regret the riches of the former possession, but the island was a threat along the sea route to North America. He sent some 80 warships under the command of his brother-in-law, General Leclerc. Toussaint was eventually defeated and shipped to France to die in captivity.

Three of his generals, Christophe, Dessalines and Pétion, continued the struggle. In the end, they turned the tide, helped by a scorched-earth policy and yellow fever, which claimed the lives of 18,000 French troops.

Independence

On January 1, 1804, Jean-Jacques Dessalines proclaimed the country independent and Saint-Domingue resumed its original name of Haiti. Dessalines became Jacques I, Emperor of Haiti, in a ceremony imitating the one at which Napoleon had himself crowned emperor of the French. His short, tyrannical rule was brought to a close by assassination in 1806. The mulattoes, an educated and powerful force, favoured Pétion as his successor, and after a struggle, he took over the south and east, while Christophe, the third of Toussaint's generals, proclaimed himself king in the north and west.

Christophe also turned tyrant, launching into a building spree that was as absurd as it was tragic. First he ordered the construction of Sans Souci palace on the hills above Milot (see p. 78), then the gargantuan fortress of Citadelle La Ferrière (see p. 79). Physical paralysis and desertion by his men forced him to one last grand gesture: in 1820 he shot himself—some say with a golden bullet.

In 1844, revolution in the eastern two-thirds of the island resulted in the formation of the Dominican Republic as a separate state. Haiti started on a long period of chaotic mismanagement, unrest and internal strife.

Modern Times

In 1915 the United States, intent on protecting the Panama Canal from Germany and preventing an accumulation of European forces in the Caribbean, sent in the marines and occupied the country. A few years of relative calm were followed by the Cacos War (1918–22), a period of guerrilla warfare. The Americans left in 1934.

Dumarsais Estimé, president from 1946 to 1950, was responsible for cleaning up the Port-au-Prince waterfront and for discharging Haiti's financial debt to the United States. But he was forced out of office and Paul Magloire, the next president, left Haiti bankrupt and in shambles.

François Duvalier, a country doctor elected president in 1957, completely changed the social fabric of the country. He derived his support from the black masses—urban and peasant—as opposed to the mulatto bourgeoisie who had held the reins of power since independence. "Papa Doc" governed Haiti until his death in 1971, relying heavily on the army and his secret police, the Tontons-Macoutes, to maintain order.

Duvalier's title of President for Life passed to his son, Jean-Claude, nicknamed "Baby Doc", who fled the country in February 1986.

Haiti has a proud history, a sadly mangled past and grave needs for the future, which it faces with faith and hope in the continuing assistance of more developed countries.

Port-au-Prince

This is the capital city with an estimated population of 900,000. It lies in a rough triangle at the point where the Cul-de-Sac plain emerges from the mountains, overlooking the Gonave Gulf.

Port-au-Prince's most important landmark, clearly visible from the sea, is the **Palais National.** Built in 1918, and modelled after the Capitol in Washington, it contains the

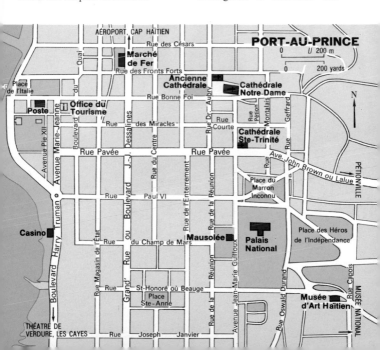

offices and apartments of the president and his family. Adjacent is the large open area of the Place des Héros de l'Indépendance, generally known as the Champ de Mars (many squares and streets in Haiti have two names, an official and a popular one), with statues of the national heroes—

Albert Mangonès's superb bronze statue of the Unknown Slave is set in the square in front of Haiti's imposing Presidential Palace.

Dessalines, Henri Christophe and Alexandre Pétion (see pp. 65–66). Directly in front lies the Place du Marron Inconnu (Square of the Unknown Slave) with Albert Mangonès' fine **statue** of a man, holding a conch shell to his lips to call his brothers to revolution.

Nearby, in the **Musée du**

Panthéon National, an underground crypt shelters the remains of the founding fathers of Haiti. Beyond the impressive modern vault are exhibited early Haitian relics, portraits and historical documents. Among them are the anchor from Columbus' ship, the *Santa Maria,* Toussaint-Louverture's elaborate watch and the silver pistol with which King Henri Christophe killed himself.

Administrative offices surround the area. Haiti has developed the unusual and practical habit of colour-coding its buildings. Yellow indicates the army, a green roof points out government buildings. The large yellow edifice to the right of the statue as you look towards the palace is the François Duvalier barracks.

A few blocks north is the Anglican **Cathédrale Sainte-Trinité** filled with murals by Haitian painters. Two Americans—Dewitt Peters, an English teacher and water colourist, and Selden Rodman, writer and critic—were instrumental in the extraordinary burgeoning of Haitian art in the '40s. Directors of the Centre d'Art in Port-au-Prince, they persuaded the Anglican bishop, Alfred Voegeli, to let Haitian **69** artists decorate the interior of his church with **biblical murals.** The results are astonishing: Philomé Obin, Rigaud Benoît, Castera-Bazile and Gabriel Levêque all produced moving religious painting; Wilson Bigaud's *Marriage at Cana*, steeped in an eerie green light, is a masterly mixture of Christian and Haitian symbolism.

Once you've seen the Sainte-Trinité murals, you will probably want to explore Haitian art further. The **Musée d'Art Haïtien** behind the Presidential Palace on the Place des Héros displays many leading Haitian artists. The shop at the back of the gallery sells interesting objects, such as wood carvings, iron sculpture, weaving and dolls.

Two other prominent churches in Port-au-Prince are La Cathédrale Notre-Dame, the official religious centre of Haiti, and l'Ancienne Cathédrale Catholique, built in 1720 under French rule.

The city's second major landmark is the so-called **Marché de Fer** (Iron Market), a fantastic construction in red and green, topped by minaret-style cupolas. It is situated downtown on Boulevard Jean-Jacques Dessalines, usually referred to as Grand'Rue. The

story goes that the structure was ordered for an oriental city, built in France by the same engineers responsible for the Eiffel Tower and then shipped to the wrong place. Be that as it may, the colourful market is a beehive of activity where you can buy just about anything from pimentoes to shoe-laces, from naïve paintings to live chickens. It's hot, noisy, smelly and fun. Incidentally, you are expected to haggle.

West are the International Exhibition Grounds, the modern centre of Port-au-Prince with offices, airlines and post office set near the harbour and edged by Truman Boulevard. The International Casino is situated here, so is the Tourist Office and the Théâtre de Verdure, where dance troupes perform twice a week. There is also a *gaguère* or cockpit and a civic fountain, prettily lit at night. The whole area is popular with Haitians for a quiet stroll in the cool of the evening.

Casino Pier on the waterfront is the departure point for daily trips to **Sand Cay Reef,** and the Beau Rivage Marina has an excursion daily to LE GRAND BAC, where there is excellent swimming and snorkelling.

A colourful phenomenon around Port-au-Prince—"tap-tap" buses look for all the world like circus wagons. Covered with paintings and symbols, each proudly bears a pious message, like "Heart of Jesus" or "The Eternal is very big". If you ride one, you have to bang twice (tap-tap) to get off.

Pétionville and Beyond

The fresh vegetables which seem like a miracle in the hot, crowded atmosphere of Port-au-Prince, have been carried down in baskets from the high country above the city.

Avenue John Brown—also known as Lalue or, more simply still, "the Pétionville road" —leads there. Along the road you'll find examples of "gingerbread" houses, neo-Gothic-looking constructions built for the richer members of Haitian society at the beginning of this century. There is also a good deal of traffic, including a steady procession of market women (in local parlance, a "Madame Sarah") carrying loads of vegetables on their heads. They start off as early as 4 in the morning to arrive in good time at the market and in the evenings you see them again, taking the other direction with their empty baskets,

moving with the peculiar, graceful swinging stride you begin to associate with Haitian people.

With its cooler temperatures and welcome breezes, **Pétionville** is where most of the richer citizens of Port-au-Prince live. It's also the location of some of Haiti's finest hotels and restaurants, as well as of many galleries selling paintings and carvings and the Haiti perfume factory.

Pétionville Square is also known as Place Saint-Pierre, after the church of Saint-Pierre set slightly to one side. From here the road goes to BOUTILLIER where the **Jane Barbancourt castle** is situated. This ersatz château containing old copper distillery vats offers free samples of various rum liqueurs.

Further on, at 3,000 feet, is a lookout point offering a superb **view** of Port-au-Prince and as far east as the ETANG SAUMÂTRE, the brackish, alligator-infested lake on the border of the Dominican Republic.

In **Kenscoff** (about 5,000 ft.), the air is so cool that you may need a sweater. Poinsettias line the road. Flowers and vegetables are grown in quantity in the area, garden produce of a temperate climate thriving in small hillside patches.

Still higher up, winding along a poor road best suited to jeeps is **Furcy,** where the air is so clean, the silence so complete and the scent of the pine trees so strong in the mountain air, you could imagine yourself in the Swiss Alps. Floating in a distant blue haze that lends mystery to many aspects of Haiti is Pic de la Selle, the country's highest peak.

Jacmel

This delightful town, set on Haiti's south coast, is about two hours by car from Port-au-Prince. It's an old colonial settlement that grew rich from the export of coffee.

Although Jacmel was swept by fire in 1893, many architectural monuments of its days of glory survive. There are magnificent houses of the coffee barons, built in the late 19th century, using ironwork shipped out as ballast on freighters from Europe. The graceful, cast-iron tendrils and whorls, seen all over town, are complemented by coloured tiles on floors and walls. Jacmel still exports coffee to Eu-

Neo-classical architecture, oddly at home under the tropical sun.

rope and the United States, and the surrounding area produces vetiver oil for the perfume industry and orange peel for the manufacture of liqueurs. But Jacmel is no longer a great export centre. Tourists are beginning to discover it—so far, only in limited numbers.

Some Haitian hotels are worth visits on their own merits. The Pension Craft in Jacmel—a rambling old building of great appeal, furnished with Haitian handicraft—is one of these. See also the Marché de Fer, less crowded than the one in Port-au-Prince but almost as grand, and the good art galleries.

Near the town are three blue lakes, known as **Les Bassins Bleus,** with tumbling waterfalls. The upper one is reputedly guarded by La Sirène, the goddess of water. She is supposed to have lost a comb from her hair in these turquoise depths and should you find it, good fortune and wealth will, of course, be yours. The lakes can be reached on foot or by horse. It's a long way ($1\frac{1}{2}$ hours on horseback), but there are superb views.

Jacmel has a rather unusual black sand beach, Congo. Other pleasant beaches stretch eastward along the south coast, but they are not easy to reach by car. CYVADIER is a little cove with the sea breaking high on rocks and a freshwater spring. RAYMOND-LES-BAINS carries memories of better times, with the remains of a promenade and old benches set by the sea. The sand is dark and rough. You have to ford a stream to get to the third beach (in rainy weather, don't risk the trip). When you do arrive, **Ti-Mouillage** ("little anchorage") beach is long and sandy, backed by a grove of coconut palms. There are no tourist facilities and you are likely to be the only visitor. Less hardy souls are advised to stay on Congo Beach until the route is improved.

West and North from Port-au-Prince

Heading west from Port-au-Prince, you come to TAÏNO BEACH, about an hour from town. The picturesque village of PETIT-GOÂVE is situated just by it and out in the bay is **Ile de la Gonâve.** Boat excursions go to this island where there is good diving and swimming.

After Taïno, a good road leads on to the town of Cayes, about $2\frac{1}{2}$ hours farther on.

Rice and yams are grown in quantity along the way.

LES CAYES, one of Haiti's larger towns, is not a particularly pretty or interesting place. However, it has a fishing fleet which puts out to sea in strange, dhow-like vessels, well worth a photograph at sunset. At CAMP-PERRIN, a hamlet near Cayes, you can, with luck, hire horses to visit

Legend has it that a siren lives here and you have only to find her comb to gain eternal happiness and wealth. Anything is possible in Haiti.

Saut Mathurine. If the horses are not forthcoming, go part of the way by car and finish off the excursion on foot. Good-natured locals will no doubt accompany you out of friendly curiosity and offer to carry your things for a small sum. The waterfall itself, a fairsized cascade tumbling into a freshwater pool, offers cool, refreshing swimming.

From Cayes, you can continue on to PORT SALUT and **Macaya Beach,** where things are much more organized for visitors. (Many people charter a plane to get there.) Macaya is not recommended for snorkelling or scuba—you have to go a long way to see anything because the fine sand turns the water milky—but the beach itself is long and lazy and absurdly empty considering the facilities of the hotel. When the tide is right, you can wade out to the little offshore island, ILE DE POINTE-SABLE and feel like a real Robinson Crusoe.

North of Port-au-Prince, all along the west coast, you'll find one curve of sand after another. The first, about 35 minutes north of the capital, is **Ibo Beach.** It has the added attraction of being set on CACIQUE ISLAND, a 5-minute launch trip from the mainland through the wandering streams of a mangrove swamp.

It's the perfect day excursion and, for this reason, very crowded on weekends. In the high season, there is a bus which goes in the morning and returns in the evening (inquire at your hotel). Ibo has everything, from lockers, changing rooms and showers to saltwater pools, facilities for water sports, minigolf, restaurants and boutiques. At night, the lights of Port-au-Prince wink across the water.

Further north, about an hour away from the city, is **Kyona Beach,** with sheltered areas for topless or nude bathing. Trips can be arranged

A tap-tap is a means of transport and a picture-book on wheels. They get you where you're going, but life is much more pleasant in a boat.

from here to the ARCADINS islands, 30 minutes away by boat, where there is excellent snorkelling and diving.

Next comes KALOA, with good water sports, and then OUANGA BAY, near the fishing village of LULLY. Local fishermen bring in the fine lobsters and fresh fish served there. A few miles farther up, XARAGUA has the only hotel in Haiti powered by solar energy. From here, too, there are trips to the Arcadins and a day excursion is offered to ILE DE LA GONÂVE. AMANI-Y-LES-BAINS, not particularly a swimmers' beach, features some of the most spectacular diving in the Caribbean.

Cap Haitien

"Cap", as it is known, is one of the most fascinating towns in Haiti. Whether you fly or drive, plan on at least three days—one for getting there, one going to Milot to visit Sans Souci and the Citadelle and one to return to Port-au-Prince. Better yet, allow extra time to take in "Cap" as well.

"Cap" itself is fairly quiet with some interesting architecture and good galleries. Haiti's most historic city, it was one of the gayest and richest places in the world under the French. A renovation programme has endowed it with a good airport, a waterfront promenade and paved streets without destroying the old-world appeal.

To reach Sans Souci palace and the Citadelle, you drive about 10 miles to the village of MILOT. You should start early, at about 7 or 8 a.m. since tropical rain clouds gather over the mountains later on. The monuments close at 6 p.m. Wear strong shoes, jeans, and take a sweater and a hat. Also remember your film. The only thing you can buy at the Citadelle is soft drinks.

Sans Souci palace has been allowed to fall into ruins, which only adds to its strange beauty. Built of brick and originally overlaid with stucco, it was three storeys high and, with dependent buildings, sentry boxes and stables, covered some 20 acres. Now reminiscent of a gigantic stage set with a magnificent double staircase, the lovely rose brick is crumbling to dust.

Henri Christophe, who ordered the construction, saw it as a new Versailles modelled after Frederick the Great's Sans Souci in Potsdam. In its heyday the palace was filled with mirrors. Gobelin tapestries, furniture and paintings. Crystal chandeliers sparkled from the ceilings. The floors were of marble and the inner walls were lined with native mahogany. A series of conduits under the lower floor carried the cool waters of a mountain stream—an early attempt at air-conditioning—which emerged as a decorative fountain.

Getting to the **Citadelle** involves a bone-shattering, 15-minute drive from Sans Souci to a car park; from there you mount on foot or by horseback. Horse hire includes the services of at least three Haitians, one to lead the horse, one to hold you on and one to hang onto the tail and provide encouraging noises. It is not an easy journey and is not recommended for elderly people. Guides are available at your hotel, at the airport and in the car park.

The constant drizzle over the mountains makes the whole experience even more extraordinary. As you approach, the Citadelle seems to hang in the grey air like a haunted battleship, spotted with the rusty lichen they call "Christophe's blood". It is justifiably known as "the eighth wonder of the world".

Started shortly after independence to repulse possible invasion by the French, the fortress was built by 200,000 ex-slaves. The herculean task included dragging building materials up the steep slopes to a height of 3,000 feet; 20,000 people are supposed to have lost their lives in the effort. Most of the work was completed by 1813.

Cannons, English, French and Spanish in origin, line the battlements. So do a number of smaller guns. Not one was ever fired in battle. Cannon balls lie in sweating piles on the damp stones. There are four galleries loaded with such ammunition. Underneath the fort are storehouses, cisterns and dungeons. Enough provisions were stocked to furnish the garrison for a year's siege. A suite of 40 rooms was maintained for the king, his family and aides. The Citadelle could house 2,000 men.

At the summit is the **upper court** from which you can see the mountains and valleys of Haiti in all their magnificence. Here Christophe, in a burst of megalomania, is supposed to have ordered a troop of soldiers to march over the parapet into the nothingness beyond to impress an English visitor.

Whether true or not, the Citadelle is a monument to the man's vanity. His tomb lies in the centre of the fortress with the inscription "Here lies King Christophe, born October 6, 1767, died October 20, 1820, whose motto is 'I am reborn from my ashes'".

Back in Cap Haitien there is another fort which can be visited, **Fort Picolet,** built by the French. Louis XIV's military engineer Vauban is supposed to have drawn the original plans. Though not on a par with the Citadelle, it's interesting for those who want to see something of the French colonial period. So, too, is the palace of Pauline Bonaparte, Napoleon's sister. She accompanied her husband, General Leclerc, on his ill-fated expedition to Haiti. The mansion lies in ruins in the rue Pauline Bonaparte; ask directions.

There are fine, but not very accessible beaches west of the town. The two easiest are **Cormier,** with a good hotel and tourist facilities and **Coco Beach,** which has no facilities but beautiful sea and sand.

At Coco Beach you can pay a local boatman to take you across the bay to LABADIE, one of the more remote Haitian villages. Don't feel it's racism if the villagers there call out "*Bonjour blanc!*" when they see you. *Blanc* (white) simply means "stranger".

What to Do

Sports. The large beach hotels north of Port-au-Prince on the west coast as well as the ones at Port Salut and Cormier offer a wide range of facilities—such as swimming pools, tennis courts, sunfish or sailfish for hire, snorkelling and scuba. From Ibo Beach there are diving excursions with instructors to Amani-y-les-Bains and the Arcadins islands, "some of the most spectacular dives in the world". On the south coast the seas are too heavy, except around Ile à Vache. Experienced divers with their own gear can explore the wrecks in the north near Cap Haitien.

And two Port-au-Prince tours give beginners a chance to view a bit of underwater life. At Sand Cay, you can see the sights from a glass-bottomed boat, don flippers and mask and investigate for yourself or, if you're not ready for that, lie supported in rubber inner tubes and be towed to where the action is. The Yellowbird excursion also involves snorkelling.

Gentle-eyed animals populate a Haitian painter's naïve vision of peace in the Garden of Eden.

Voodoo

Not "black magic" at all but an animistic religion from Africa, voodoo exists side by side with Christianity in Haiti. Often Catholic saints have voodoo counterparts.

A voodoo ceremony may last from a few hours to a few days and is led by a *hougan* (priest) or *mambo* (priestess) assisted by *hounsi*. It's held in a *péristyle* (courtyard). They dance and sing with frenetic energy to the tireless beat of a drum.

Before the ceremony, line patterns or *vévés* are drawn on the floor in corn flour or ashes to summon the *loas* (spirits). In an atmosphere of increasing noise and excitement, glowing branches may be pulled from the fire and eaten as one of the *loas* takes possession of an individual and is recognized.

Though few visitors will have an opportunity to witness a "real" voodoo ceremony, the touristic version is not unauthentic.

Shopping. Undoubtedly, it's the **paintings** and **carvings** that will catch your eye, as well as metal sculptures cut from the tops of oil drums. There are dozens of galleries, some famous and selling the work of well-known artists, but all with something attractive.

The beautiful **craft work** includes basketry, embroidery, inlaid woodwork, inlaid horn work and small pieces of furniture. Around Jacmel, look for embroidered dresses, shirts, and tablecloths that would embellish a royal banquet. Also to be considered as souvenirs, **rum** and rum liqueurs.

Entertainment. By night there are the usual nightclubs, discotheques and folklore shows at the hotels. Haiti's national dance, by the way, is the *méringue*. Haitian rhythm reaches its peak at Carnival time before Ash Wednesday.

You will also find French-dubbed cinema for film fans and casinos for gamblers. By day, there are the cockfights at the *gaguère* in Port-au-Prince or simply cropping up around the countryside. Ask at your hotel.

By day it's cool drinks. Night brings the disturbing beat of the drums, dance and strange gods.

Almost every visitor wants to attend a voodoo ceremony in Haiti. The elaborate ritual complete with *vévé* symbols, dancing and singing is staged for the public.

Wining and Dining. Creole cooking is delicious, a combination of tropical ingredients and French flair. There are plenty of crayfish, delicate, spicy ways of preparing other fish, *lambi* (the local word for conch), plantains, served fried, and a black mushroom known

as *djon-djon*, a luxurious addition to rice. *Griot*, a ubiquitous snack, is made of pork, first boiled, then fried in its own fat. *Mamba* is peanut butter, freshly ground. You see people making it with a huge wooden mortar and pestle and it is sometimes sold at the side of the road. Cassava bread is coarse and good, but you may have to ferret it out for yourself since it is not usually served in the hotels. Tropical fruits abound. Ordinary dessert bananas are called *figues*, soursop is *corossol* and sweetsop is *cachiment*.

To precede, there are all the cocktails of the sophisticated world with a special emphasis on rum drinks. To accompany the meal there are fine imported wines or the local beer and, to follow, liqueurs, including tropically flavoured specialities, as well as good Haitian coffee.

Haiti Briefing

Airports. Port-au-Prince's François Duvalier International Airport (13 kilometres/8 miles east of the city centre) is the main point of entry. A small airport departure tax is charged when leaving the country.

Car hire and driving. Car hire firms operate at François Duvalier Airport, in Port-au-Prince and Pétionville. A valid U.S., Canadian or international driving licence is required. Drive on the right. Keep the speed down, and use your horn to warn pedestrians of your approach. Highways connect Port-au-Prince with Cap Haitien and with Les Cayes. Secondary roads are often extremely difficult—inquire about road conditions at the hotel or tourist office before setting out.

Currency. The unit of currency is the *gourde,* divided into 100 *centimes.* The gourde has been pegged to the American dollar since 1919. Prices are tagged in dollars, which are accepted everywhere at a fixed rate of 5 gourdes to the dollar. Payment can also be made in traveller's cheques or by credit card in most hotels and larger shops.

Electric current. 110 volts, 60 cycles, A.C.

Entry regulations. U.S. and Canadian nationals require proof of citizenship as well as an onward or return ticket. All other nationalities need a passport, and some, a visa.

Health. In hotels and tourist restaurants, the water supplied in carafes is perfectly safe. Do not drink tap water and do not drink from streams or rivers. All hotels have doctors on call.

Hotels. Mainly top and luxury class. Bills include a 10% service charge and a 5% government tax. Hotel porters and bellboys expect a small tip.

Hours. Shops: 8 a.m.–4 p.m. in summer, till 5 p.m. in winter, Monday to Friday; 8 a.m.–12 noon or 2 p.m. on Saturdays. Banks: 9 a.m.–1 p.m., Monday to Friday.

Public holidays. Jan. 1 (Independence Day and New Year's Day), Jan. 2 (Forefathers' Day), Carnival (three days preceding Ash Wednesday), Good Friday (movable), April 14 (Pan American Day), May 1 (Labour Day), Ascension (movable), May 18 (Flag and University Day), May 22 (Sovereignty Day), Corpus Christi (movable), June 22 (National Thanksgiving), Aug. 15 (Assumption Day), Oct. 17 (Dessaline's Death Anniversary), Oct. 24 (U.N. Day), Nov. 1 (All Saints' Day), Nov. 2 (All Soul's Day), Nov. 18 (Armed Forces Day), Dec. 5 (Discovery Day), Dec. 25 (Christmas Day).

Time. Haiti is on EST (5 hours behind GMT) throughout the year.

Tourist information offices

Haiti: Government Tourist Bureau *(Office National du Tourisme)*, Avenue Marie-Jeanne, Port-au-Prince; tel. 2-1729

Canada: 44 Fundy, Floor F, Place Bonaventure, Montreal, Que. H5A 1A9; tel. (514) 871-9897
920 Yonge Street, Suite 808, Toronto, Ont. M4W 3C7; tel. (416) 923-7833

U.S.A.: 5959 West Loop South, Suite 500, Bellaire (Houston), TX 77401; tel. (713) 666-0931
919 North Michigan Avenue, Chicago, IL 60611; tel. (312) 337-1603
7100 Biscayne Boulevard, Miami, FL 33138; tel. (305) 758-8760
30 Rockefeller Plaza, New York, NY 10020; tel. (212) 757-3517

France: Regional European Office, 64 rue la Boétie, 75008 Paris; tel. 45.63.66.97

Transport. Taxis are the most convenient means of local transport. They are not metered, so agree on the price before you start off (your hotel receptionist will advise you). It is not customary to tip taxi drivers. *Publiques* (group taxis), *camionnettes* (open minibuses with benches) and *tap-taps* (brightly painted trucks with benches) are very inexpensive, but for the more adventurous only.

Dominican Republic

The Dominican Republic, an independent country, covers the eastern two-thirds of the island of Hispaniola. Two mountain ranges, the Cordillera Central and the Cordillera Septentrional, stretch across the land, cradling fertile valleys. The remainder is hills and lowlands with Pico Duarte, the highest peak in the West Indies, towering to 10,000 feet.

High unemployment and recession have hit the Dominican Republic, one of the most stable and productive Latin-American countries. Dominican exports include sugar, cacao and bauxite. The amber deposits are the world's largest.

The capital of Santo Domingo, the oldest city in the New World, is packed with history. Near La Romana in the south and Puerto Plata in the north, beautiful sweeps of sandy beach, endowed with a full complement of luxurious amenities, attract tourists. Visitors will be impressed by the air of cleanliness and prosperity.

There is a strong pro-American feeling which finds expression in the Dominican passion for basketball and baseball. Many in the tourist industry speak some English, but it would be a good idea to brush up on your Spanish before your trip—for language can be a problem.

Christopher Columbus discovered the island in 1492 when it was still populated by the Taino Indians. His brother served as governor and his

son, Diego, as viceroy. Splendid buildings were constructed, and the colony flourished. But gradually Spain's interest drifted to the richer lands of South America, and Santo Domingo fell into neglect. When Sir Francis Drake took the town in 1586, it was too poor to pay the ransom he optimistically demanded, so he set fire to it.

The following centuries saw brief domination by the French, revolts leading to independence, Spanish rule

Spain has left its imprint on the historic streets of Santo Domingo.

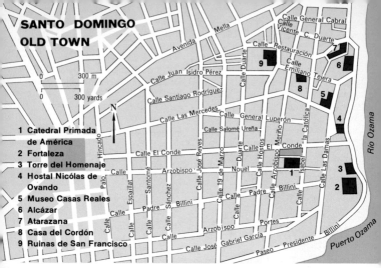

SANTO DOMINGO OLD TOWN

0   300 m
0   300 yards

N

1 Catedral Primada de América
2 Fortaleza
3 Torre del Homenaje
4 Hostal Nicólas de Ovando
5 Museo Casas Reales
6 Alcázar
7 Atarazana
8 Casa del Cordón
9 Ruinas de San Francisco

Map labels: Calle General Cabral, Calle Vicente C. Duarte, Mella, Calle Restauración, Avenida, Calle Emiliano Tejera, Calle Juan Isidro Pérez, Calle Duarte, Calle Santiago Rodríguez, Calle Las Mercedes, Calle General Luperón, Calle Salomé Ureña, Calle El Conde, Hincado, Calle, Calle José Reyes, Arzobispo, Calle 19 de Marzo, Calle José Sánchez, Nouel, Calle Padre Billini, Calle Hostos, El Conde, Calle Arzobispo Meriño, Isabel la Católica, Calle Las Damas, Arzobispo, Portes, Billini, Calle José Gabriel García, Paseo — Presidente, Espaillat, Santomé, Palo, Río Ozama, Puerto Ozama

again, then a period of Haitian control until finally, in 1844, another revolt, and independence—but not stability—was re-achieved.

The U.S. Marines occupied the country in 1916 and didn't leave until 1924. General Trujillo came to power in 1930. His dictatorship lasted until his assassination more than 30 years later. Instability and then civil war resulted in a second American military intervention in 1965. Today this democratic republic of about 6 million people is governed by a president, senate and chamber of deputies, with free elections **88** every four years.

Santo Domingo

Although much of this city of over 1 million is vibrantly modern, the **old town** contains monuments of unique historical interest.

Central point is the **Catedral Primada de América,** Santa María la Menor, the oldest cathedral in the New World. Completed in 1540, the exterior is Renaissance and the interior contains Gothic vaulting. The main entrance has a huge door, weighing $2\frac{1}{2}$ tons, that dates back to the founding of the cathedral.

Inside you'll find the reputed remains of Christopher Columbus in a massive **mauso-**

leum of marble and bronze topped with a bronze statue. They open the tomb once a year, on October 12, the anniversary of the explorer's discovery of the New World.

In the first chapel to the right of the altar, Francis Drake slung his hammock and slept during his stay in 1586. You can see where he maliciously chipped the nose off a statue.

The Chapel of the Holy Sacrament contains a superb baroque **altar** in Dominican mahogany and silver.

Calle Las Damas, the oldest street in the city, lined with colonial buildings, is named after the ladies-in-waiting of María de Toledo, Columbus' daughter-in-law. It leads to the Fortaleza Ozama (fortress), dominated by the imposing **Torre del Homenaje** (Tower of Homage). Constructed at the beginning of the 16th century, this square, no-nonsense building contains a wooden spiral staircase. Ships entering the harbour used to be saluted from here—whence the name. The fortress is supposed to be haunted. It certainly looks grim enough.

Heading north on Calle Las Damas, you pass the **Hostal Nicolás de Ovando** on your right, a fine 16th-century

house incorporated within a hotel. The door is considered an admirable example of Isabelline Gothic.

The **Museo de las Casas Reales** (Royal Houses Museum) is diagonally across Calle Las Damas. Note the exquisite entrance with the heraldic shield of Emperor Charles V. The museum merits a visit for its excellent material on Dominican history from earliest times, including Indian relics and models of Columbus' ships.

The **Alcázar** (castle) stands on a slight rise. It was built about 1510 for Diego Columbus. When the Columbus family died out in Santo Domingo, the Alcázar fell to ruin. Now well restored, it houses a first-class museum with furniture, tapestries, paintings, musical instruments and a very fine 16th-century Flemish carving of the *Death of the Virgin.*

The **Atarazana,** just beyond, consists of eight 16th-century buildings—an early New World trade centre. Now galleries, boutiques and restaurants have moved into this charming colonial neighbourhood.

Sculpted in stone over the entrance to the **Casa del Cordón** (House of the Cord) is the belt of St. Francis. It was here that rich women of the city brought their jewels to have them weighed as a contribution to the ransom demanded by Francis Drake.

At the end of Calle Emiliano Tejera are the **Ruinas de San Francisco,** probably the oldest monastery in the New World. Its dedication to St. Francis is marked, again, by a gracefully carved replica of the white cord of the order.

The modern city has an entirely different atmosphere. Startingly up-to-date buildings decorate the **Plaza de la Cultura.** Among them is the marble and mahogany Teatro Nacional and the grey, corrugated Galería de Arte Moderno (Museum of Modern Art). A forest of contemporary statuary rises in front of it. Well worth a visit, the **Museo del Hombre Dominicano** (Museum of the Dominican Man) has a good collection of pre-Columbian artefacts, necklaces, ornaments and amulets, as well as objects from the colonial period.

On the edge of the city to the north are the **botanical gardens,** one of the world's largest, featuring tropical plants

Old architecture, young people reflect the same simple grace.

and flowers and a Japanese park; the nearby **zoo** has an enormous open-air cage housing some 4,000 birds.

An agreeable short trip (about 20 minutes by road) on the way to the airport brings you to **Los Tres Ojos de Agua** (The Three Eyes of Water), a group of turquoise pools in a natural underground rock formation, complete with stalactites and stalagmites.

Further south-east begins a series of fine beaches with shallow water and soft sands. **Boca Chica,** close to the airport, is the first of them, followed by **Juan Dolio** and **Guayacanes.**

La Romana

The industry around these parts used to be sugar. Nowadays, although the sugar mill —one of the largest in the world—is still flourishing and can be visited, La Romana is far more likely to be identified with the Dominican Republic's tourist industry. It's 112 kilometres from Santo Domingo and even has its own jet strip.

A huge, beautifully planned tourist complex is developing nearby—**Casa de Campo.** The beaches are good, but there is a great deal besides beach: celebrated riding stables, polo, fine swimming pools, fishing and water-sport tournaments, a tennis village, a golf village and two professional golf courses already eliciting superlatives.

Altos de Chavón, set on a plateau and offering views of the Chavón River, is an artists' village built in imitation of 15th-century Spain, especially created as a setting for musicians, painters and writers from the Dominican Republic and abroad.

The North

The excellent highway to the north coast runs near the towns of CONSTANZA and JARABACOA, set in the cool Cordillera mountains.

Santiago, or Santiago de los Treinta Caballeros to give it its full, dashing name, is the country's second largest city (pop. 350,000), capital of the fertile El Cibao region. Thirty noblemen founded the town and named it after their patron saint, St. James. In 1562 it was destroyed by an earthquake, but not before a mysterious friar had appeared and warned all just men to leave.

Santiago is a centre for music and dance and the popular *merengue* may have originated here, influenced by the rhythms of early Spanish music.

Swim up for a drink. The floating bar at the Casa de Campo pool features cool, on-the-spot service.

Puerto Plata on the country's Amber Coast has some of the most enticing beaches you could ever hope to find. It is riding the crest of a tourist boom and has its own international airport. Cruise-ship passengers enter under the walls of the fortress **San Felipe,** built to guard the country from Carib Indians and British pirates. Like most of the country's 16th-century monuments, it has been well restored.

One of the many appealing features of Puerto Plata is its architecture, a blend of Spanish colonial and Victorian. Columbus gave the town its name, which means "port of

silver" and brought sugar cane plants.

Fields of the sugar cane, with their waving "flags" or flowers, now surround Puerto Plata. The area is also noted for the amber mines that produce the resin worked into jewellery and ornaments for sale throughout the country. Its colours range from almost crystalline to very dark brown.

Take one of the red cable-cars up to the top of the Isabel de Torres mountain (2,565 ft.) where a giant statue of Christ the Redeemer stretches protective arms over city and harbour.

East a little is **Playa Dorada** with great golfing on a Robert Trent course and luxurious tourist facilities. Further east lies **Sosúa,** on a lovely bay settled by Jewish refugees in the 1930s. The town has a flourishing smoked meat and dairy industry. Call in, too, at Río San Juan to explore the **Gri Gri Lagoon** by boat. **Playa Grande,** a luxury resort area, was a twin project to Playa Dorada. Ten holes of the Robert Trent course front the Atlantic.

Live chickens for sale are part of everyday business in Santiago.

Samaná is a charming fishing port even further east, whose 7,000-strong population is English-speaking. This peninsula, long isolated geographically from the rest of the country, is home to descendants of fugitive American slaves. They arrived via Pennsylvania in 1824 and still use the antiquated English of their forebears, with a caressing Southern accent.

What to Do

Sports. There is swimming and sunbathing, of course, with the diving and snorkelling very good around La Caleta; boating and sailing at Santo Domingo and La Romana; deep-sea fishing, especially at La Romana, Barahona, Puerto Plata and Samaná.

There are outstanding facilities for tennis in all the tourist centres and golf at Santo Domingo Country Club, two 18-hole courses at La Romana and 9-hole courses in Puerto Plata and Jarabacoa. If you're really serious, you can even live in a tennis or golf village.

The Spanish tradition of horsemanship continues and there are fine mounts and various exhibitions and tournaments. Horse fans will find polo fields at Sierra Prieta in Santo Domingo and Casa de **95**

Baseball is the most popular, but there is also basketball, boxing, horse-racing and cock-fighting.

Shopping. Carving and weaving are part of the country's tradition and mahogany, one of its treasures. Of special interest for visitors is the jewellery made from amber (found here in very large quantities) or from larimar, the "Dominican turquoise", an attractive blue stone often combined with silver.

Eating and Entertainment. There's a Spanish flavour to everything, from the *merengue* music to the clothes (neat and elegant) and food.

Some typical snacks to pick up along the way are *quipes*, a type of sandwich of Arab origin, *catibias*, fried yucca, and *pastelitos*, meat patties which become fish patties during Lent. All the lush fruit of the Caribbean is there for your enjoyment. A popular sweet is *dulce de leche*, made from milk.

After dinner possibilities include nightclubs and cocktail lounges with live entertainment and gambling. Santo Domingo has four casinos. If you play in pesos, your winnings are paid in pesos; if you play in dollars, you're repaid in dollars.

Campo in La Romana; Playa Dorada has a riding school. Riding trails are being incorporated at Playa Grande.

Pigeon hunting is a popular sport from July to October. For information, contact the Tourist Office.

Spectator sports abound, mostly with an American bias.

Dominican Republic Briefing

Airports. There are two international airports, Aeropuerto Internacional de las Américas, serving Santo Domingo (a 25-minute drive from the city), and Aeropuerto Internacional La Union on the north coast for the Puerto Plata/Playa Dorada/Sosúa areas (a 20-minute drive east of Puerto Plata, 15 minutes west of Sosúa).

On leaving the Dominican Republic, visitors must pay an airport departure tax.

Car hire and driving. Various international and local car hire firms have offices at Las Américas International Airport as well as in the capital. Some arrangements include mileage. Your home licence is valid for up to 90 days. Drive on the right. Service stations are open from 6 a.m. to 6 p.m. daily.

Currency. The Dominican *peso* is divided into 100 *centavos*. It is illegal to change currency at places other than banks or hotels. Export of local currency is prohibited. Traveller's cheques and credit cards are accepted in hotels, restaurants and a great number of shops.

Electric current. 110 volts, 60 cycles, A.C.

Entry regulations. U.S. and Canadian nationals require proof of citizenship (but it is advisable to have a valid passport) and a tourist card, obtainable from the airline they fly with. All other nationalities need a passport. Visas are not required of British and most other Western European visitors.

Health. Do not drink tap water; the drinking water provided in hotels and tourist restaurants is safe, but avoid water in small local restaurants.

Hotels. All categories are catered for, and at some beaches there are cottages for rent. Bills include a 10% service charge and 5% government tax. Hotel porters and bellboys expect a small tip.

Hours. Shops: 8.30 a.m.–12 noon and 2.30–6 p.m., Monday to Saturday. Offices: 8 a.m.–12 noon and 2–6 p.m., Monday–Friday. Banks: 8 a.m.–12.30 p.m.

Public holidays. Jan. 1 (New Year's Day), Jan. 21 (Our Lady of Altagracia's Day), Jan. 26 (Duarte's Birthday), Feb. 27 (Independence Day), Good Friday (movable), May 1 (Labour Day), Corpus Christi (movable), Aug. 16 (Restoration Day), Sept. 24 (Feast of Our Lady of Mercy), Dec. 25 (Christmas Day).

Time. The Dominican Republic is on Atlantic Standard Time (EST + 1, GMT − 4) all year round.

Tourist information offices

The Dominican Republic: Dominican Tourist Information Center *(Centro Dominicano de Información Turística)*, Calle Arzobispo Meriño 156, Santo Domingo; tel. 685-3282

U.S.A.: 2355 Sanzedo Street, Suite 305, Coral Gables, FL 33134; tel. (305) 444-4592
548 South Spring Street, Los Angeles, CA 90013; tel. (213) 627-3414
485 Madison Avenue, New York, NY 10020; tel. (212) 826-0750
1300 Ashford Avenue, Santurce, PR 00907; tel. (809) 725-4774

West Germany: Regional European Office, Voelckerstrasse 24, D-6000 Frankfurt am Main; tel. (069) 597 03 30

Transport. Bus services in Santo Domingo are efficient and inexpensive, but often crowded. Taxis can be picked up outside most hotels or hailed on the street. Some taxis (called *públicos*) run on fixed routes in the capital and other main cities. Vehicles are not metered, and it's advisable to agree on the fare before setting off (your hotel receptionist will advise you). Taxi drivers don't expect to be tipped.

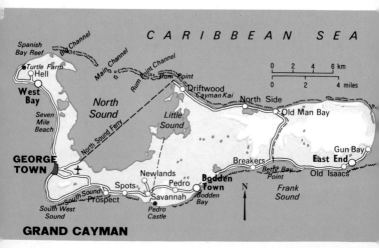

Cayman Islands

Sleepy, peaceful and British to the back teeth, the Cayman Islands dot the sea about 180 miles north-west of Jamaica. There are no cries for independence here. Things run smoothly under a governor general, Queen Elizabeth II's photograph is hung with pride on office walls and the language is English.

The Caymans, three islands of which Grand Cayman is the largest and Cayman Brac and Little Cayman the lesser members of the family, have spent most of their history quietly being ignored. This is no longer true, for tourists have discovered the beaches and the gentle atmosphere, like a small town, where everybody knows everybody else. Besides, the islands have become a financial centre—with over 400 banks. There is no income tax, no profit tax, no capital gains tax, no estate and death duties. Consequently, international business thrives here. This financial story, which began in the late 1960s, has led to tremendous economic expansion.

In spite of affluence, in spite of the tourists who now come in increasing numbers, the place has retained its sober gait. Americans feel at home, since the American influence is strong. The British may think that this is the way an English country village could be if only someone pepped up the economy and turned on the sun.

Columbus, of course, discovered these islands (in 1503), noted the "seas full of turtles" and called the group Las Tortugas. Later many ships came to these waters to collect fresh turtle meat. But for some reason, the name changed to Caymanas, the Carib word for crocodiles. The turtles remain as well-treated inhabitants in a turtle farm, but the crocodiles —they were probably iguanas anyway—are nowhere to be found.

Legend has it that the first settlers were two deserters from Cromwell's army, Bodden and Watler, names found all over the islands today. The pirates came and went, delighting in the remoteness of Grand Cayman and its absolute flatness, which makes it practically invisible against the horizon—in short, a perfect hideaway. The sea has always dominated the lives of Caymanians, who are renowned as excellent seamen.

In 1863 the islands were formally annexed to Jamaica, but **99** when Jamaica chose independence in 1962, the Caymans elected to become a British Crown Colony. Nowadays inhabitants are reckoned to have one of the highest per capita incomes in the Caribbean. Prices are high, though, since nearly everything has to be imported.

Here we concentrate on Grand Cayman, the most accessible of the Caymans.

Grand Cayman
Pop. 14,000

GEORGE TOWN (written in two words), the capital, is thriving but very quiet. There are no great sights and although it is pleasant to wander around the well-planned streets (where all the cars stop to let you pass), you will no doubt soon want to head north for **Seven Mile Beach** (they're exaggerating, it's only 6 miles, really), where the big hotels are located and clean white sand stretches to an invitingly blue sea.

Continue north along the coast road to the world's first **green turtle farm.** It provides a legal source of turtle products, such as meat, hide and tortoise shell, and aims at protecting an endangered species. You can eat turtle on Cayman without suffering pangs of ecological guilt.

Afterwards you may as well go to HELL. The name refers to the Dantesque area of black rock formations. Its major industry revolves around selling postcards and stamps and postmarking them to prove you have, indeed, been to Hell.

East of George Town, the road runs to Pedro Castle,

originally built by an Englishman who arrived in the islands in 1765. Local—unsubstantiated—stories also associate it with the pirate Henry Morgan and a 16th-century Spaniard, Pedro Gomez.

At EAST END, sprays of water shoot like geysers through the sea-torn rocks and, further on, the wrecks begin. Over 325 of them have been counted around Grand Cayman, not all the result of natural circumstances. The most southerly, off the east coast, is the

Tame pirates rove the harbour at George Town, Grand Cayman.

Ridgefield, perfectly visible from the road. Though the ship was practically empty when lured onto a reef in 1943, at least she carried the bonus of 100 cases of beer.

Grand Cayman's central road which strikes off to the left some distance after BETTY BAY POINT, takes you to the north side and then west as far as CAYMAN KAI and RUM POINT. The silky sand has been divided up and very pleasant beach houses have gone up. The whole landscape shines blue and silver, it's New England in a Caribbean setting. The gardens are beautifully planted (amazing what will grow in sand), the holiday houses verging on the luxurious.

What to Do

Sports. The swimming is good, so is the snorkelling, and the diving has a strong claim to being the best in the Caribbean. For underwater photography, head for Spanish Bay Reef where they have all the gear and expertise.

Beyond the reefs are the big fish such as bluefin, marlin and wahoo. Bonito, amberjack

Treasures under the sea. Turtle-watching is for the landlubbers.

and barracuda are closer to shore and inside the reef you will land grouper and yellow-tailed snapper. Boats can be rented, ranging from a 60-foot yacht to a dinghy. Experts say the best fishing guides are on Cayman Brac and Little Cayman.

Shopping. Duty free and offering luxury goods from worldwide sources. There's crystal, perfumes, cameras, woollens and silver.

More typical of Cayman, though, is the very elegant jewellery in coral (including black coral) often set in gold with precious stones and tortoise shell.

Entertainment. Naturally, it's quiet—which is after all part of the charm since people get to know each other—but visitors can also enjoy dining out (specialities include conch chowder, turtle steak, breadfruit puffs), dancing, discos and movies.

Once every year Caymanians honour the buccaneers with Pirate Week (usually late October). Then there are parades, banquets, treasure hunts, coconut-shucking contests and pirate ship cruises. The governor general submits to being "captured" as part of the fun, and a gala ball is held to wind it all up.

Cayman Islands Briefing

Airports. Main airport is Owen Roberts International on Grand Cayman. Domestic air services link Grand Cayman, Little Cayman and Cayman Brac.

Car hire and driving. Car hire agencies issue temporary permits on presentation of your home driving licence. Drive on the *left.*

Currency. The unit of currency is the Cayman Islands dollar, divided into 100 cents. Prices are usually quoted in Cayman dollars, but shops will also accept U.S. and Canadian dollars.

Entry regulations. British and U.S. nationals require proof of citizenship and an onward or return ticket. All other nationalities need a passport, and some a visa.

Hotels. Accommodation is quite varied—hotels, guest houses, villas, apartments—the majority on Grand Cayman. Bills include a 5% government tax, and many establishments add a 10–15% service charge.

Hours. Most shops are open from 8.30 a.m. to 5 p.m., Monday to Saturday, some supermarkets till 9 or 10 p.m. on Fridays and Saturdays. Banks: 9.30 a.m.–3 p.m., Monday to Thursday, till 5 p.m. Fridays.

Time. The Cayman Islands are on EST (GMT − 5) throughout the year.

Tourist information offices

Cayman Islands Department of Tourism: P.O. Box 67, George Town, Grand Cayman, B.W.I.; tel. 9-4844

Canada: Earl B. Smith, Travel Marketing Consultants, 11 Adelaide Street, Suite 406, Toronto, Ont. M5H 1L9; tel. (416) 362-1550

United Kingdom: Cayman Islands News Bureau, Hambleton House, 17 B Curzon Street, London W1Y 7FE; tel. (01) 493-5161

U.S.A.: 250 Catalonia Avenue, Suite 604, Coral Gables, FL 33134; tel. (305) 444-6551
333 N. Michigan Avenue, Suite 905, Chicago, IL 60601; tel. (312) 782-5832
9999 Richmond Avenue, Suite 131, Houston, TX 77042; tel. (713) 977-0604
3440 Wilshire Blvd., Suite 1202, Los Angeles, CA 90010; tel. (213) 738-1968
420 Lexington Avenue, Suite 2312, New York, NY 10017; tel. (212) 682-5582

Transport. Taxis, with fixed rates, are the most convenient means of transport. On Grand Cayman, there is also frequent bus service along Seven Mile Beach, between George Town and West Bay.

BLUEPRINT for a Perfect Trip

How to Get There

It is advisable to consult a travel agent for the latest information on tariffs and other arrangements.

BY AIR

Scheduled flights

Jamaica: Jamaica has two international airports—Norman Manley in Kingston and Donald Sangster in Montego Bay. Visitors may transfer by air to Ocho Rios, Port Antonio and other resorts by the domestic airline, Trans Jamaica, which leaves from the small Tinson Pen Airport in the heart of Kingston. All flights are scheduled. Ground transport is also extensively used.

Haiti: The main gateway to Haiti is Port-au-Prince's François Duvalier International Airport, which is served by scheduled flights mainly from North and South American cities. Daily flights connect Port-au-Prince with Cap Haitien, and there is regular service between Les Cayes on the south coast.

Dominican Republic: The Republic is served by Santo Domingo's Aeropuerto Internacional de las Américas and the Aeropuerto Internacional La Unión on the north coast. Domestic airlines have flights to other points in the country, such as La Romana and Puerto Plata.

Cayman Islands: The two main gateways are Owen Roberts International Airport on Grand Cayman and Gerrard Smith International Airport on Cayman Brac.

Charter flights and package tours

From North America: Sports programmes (golf, tennis, diving) are featured year-round, as well as honeymoon and family arrangements. Many vacation packages are offered with or without car hire. A three-night plan is available for holiday weekends. If meals are not included in your programme, the Modified American Plan (MAP—breakfast plus one other meal) is a money-saver.

From the U.K.: A variety of packages to Jamaica are featured, usually for 10 to 14 nights. Tours direct to Haiti are not available from the U.K., though some operators offer a three- to seven-day Haitian extension to a Jamaica holiday.

BY SEA

Jamaica and Haiti are popular stops on Caribbean cruises. Many operators fly tourists out to Miami, New York or Puerto Rico to join their ship.

When to Go

Except for missing the sheer pleasure of taking off to a warm climate when the weather at home is at its most dismal, there is no real reason to scorn a summer or autumn vacation in the Caribbean. Seasonal temperature differences in this part of the world are not enormous, and what extra precipitation there is during some off-season months is usually limited to a brief rain shower in the afternoon.

Average monthly temperatures and days of rain for Jamaica:

		J	F	M	A	M	J	J	A	S	O	N	D
Temperature	°C	25	25	25	26	27	28	28	28	28	27	26	25
	°F	77	77	77	79	80	82	82	82	82	80	79	77
Days of rain		5	4	4	6	7	6	6	8	10	12	8	5

Planning Your Budget

To give you an idea of what to expect, here is a rundown of average prices in Jamaican tourist areas. The Jamaican dollar is the only legal tender. For easy calculation, some of the rates given below are in U.S. dollars. All prices must be regarded as *approximate* only.

Airport departure tax. J$40.

Airport ground transfers. JUTA car from Norman Manley International Airport (Kingston) to hotels downtown or midtown in the New Kingston area J$73 per car (taking up to 5 people depending on luggage), from Donald Sangsters International Airport (Montego Bay) to the hotel strip, Gloucester Avenue, J$35, to hotels in the Rose Hall area J$67, to Negril J$308, to Runaway Bay J$308, to Ocho Rios J$392, to Port Antonio J$706.

Car hire. Rates range from U.S.$44 per day with unlimited mileage for a small car with standard shift, to U.S.$90 per day for an air-conditioned, automatic luxury car. Some firms offer lower down payments to clients with advance reservations.

Cigarettes. J$7.50–8 per packet of 20.

Hairdressers. *Woman's* shampoo, conditioning and blow-dry J$45–90. *Man's* shampoo, cut and blow-dry J$30–55.

Holiday villas (staffed). U.S.$700–4,600 per week depending on size.

Hotels (double room with bath, winter season). EP U.S.$20–80 per person per night. All inclusive U.S.$1,950–2,640 per couple per week. MAP, per person per night U.S.$150–265.

Meals (average costs, including drink and tip). In moderately priced but good establishment, lunch U.S.$5–10, dinner from U.S.$15, in luxury establishment, lunch U.S.$20–35, dinner from U.S.$40.

Taxis (un-metered; city). From the New Kingston hotel area to downtown Kingston approx. J$20–25, from Norman Manley Airport to Port Antonio or Ocho Rios approx. J$400 per car.

Trains. Kingston to Montego Bay, first class J$26 (one way), economy J$17.

Watersports. Sail fish/sun fish from U.S.$15 per hour, windsurfer U.S.$10 per hour, scuba (including all equipment) U.S.$35 per hour, glass-bottom boats U.S.$8 per person per hour, cruises U.S.$20 per person for 3 hours, deep-sea fishing (including crew and bait) U.S.$300 for 1–4 people.

An A–Z Summary of Practical Information and Facts

A star (*) following an entry indicates that relevant prices are to be found on page 108.

For practical information on Haiti, the Dominican Republic and the Cayman Islands, see pp. 84, 97 and 104 respectively.

ACCOMMODATION is subject to government inspection, and only establishments on the official Tourist Board list are approved. In Jamaica, a hotel means lodgings with more than ten rooms; otherwise it's called a guest-house.

Hotels*. Major hotels offer all the usual amenities, including air-conditioning, room service and swimming pools. More modest establishments may have a roof fan instead of air-conditioning.

Prices are higher in the tourist season (mid-December to mid-April), and booking for that period should be made well in advance. During the rest of the year, rates may be as much as 40% lower. An accommodation tax is in force. Bills and receipts issued by hotels indicate the room charge separately from other charges.

Here's a key to the various "plans" available:

AI = All Inclusive (properties with all meals and drinks plus organized leisure activities and services included. No tipping)
AP = American Plan (three meals)
MAP = Modified American Plan (breakfast and dinner)
CP = Continental Plan (breakfast only)
EP = European Plan (no meals)

Holiday villas*. If you want to get away from the hotel scene but not have the everyday housekeeping chores, you can rent a staffed villa. Arrangements usually include a cook and other household staff. Most holiday villas have a swimming pool. For details, write to:

Jamaica Association of Villas and Apartments (JAVA), Pineapple Place, Ocho Rios

AIRPORTS*. Jamaica has two international airports.

The **Norman Manley Airport** (also known as Palisadoes) is the most convenient point of entry for Kingston, Port Antonio, the eastern part

A of the island and Mandeville. A bus runs from the terminal into the capital, but most visitors prefer to cover the 10 miles by taxi, a trip of about 20 minutes. The hotel area of New Kingston is 13 miles from the airport.

The **Donald Sangster International Airport** at Montego Bay serves the north coast and the western end of the island. There are buses and plenty of taxis to make the five-minute journey into town.

Both airports are modern, with all relevant services—including restaurants, bars and small boutiques for magazines and last-minute souvenirs. Red-cap porters will handle your luggage for a fixed charge per piece; trolleys are also available. Hospitality Centres (for information) remain open for most scheduled flights. You'll have to change money at the airport to pay for the bus or taxi journey to the hotel.

An airport tax is levied for departing passengers.

B **BICYCLE and MOTORSCOOTER HIRE.** Bicycles are available free of charge at many hotels.

You can hire a two-seater 50- or 100-cc motorscooter at most resorts. Your hotel receptionist will direct you to rental agencies. An ordinary driving licence is all that is required. Crash-helmets are recommended.

Don't forget to drive on the left here. Night riding is discouraged.

C **CAMPING.** In the absence of patrolled sites, camping is discouraged. However, if you insist, you might try the approved camping sites at Negril (Negril Lighthouse Park), Montego Bay (Damali Beach Village) or Kingston (Maya).

CAR HIRE* (see also DRIVING IN JAMAICA). International and local firms have offices in the major centres—some of them in hotels—as well as at both major airports. During high season (mid-December to mid-April) it is advisable to reserve your vehicle well in advance through your travel agency at home.

Drivers must be 21 years of age and have held a licence for at least one year. Your home driving licence is recognized in Jamaica. In the 21–25 age group, a bond must be posted to comply with insurance regulations.

Differences in rates and conditions between the international and local companies are minimal. Some mileage is often included. Unless the rental period exceeds three days, a drop-off charge is applied if you wish to turn in the vehicle somewhere else on the island. Payment must be made in Jamaican dollars. Credit cards and traveller's cheques are accepted.

And, before you actually set off, don't forget you're in a left-hand-drive country.

CHILDREN. Some hotels have playrooms well stocked with toys, children's libraries, special movies and meals, and trained nannies in attendance. Ask the Jamaica Tourist Board for a list of such establishments. Your hotel will in any case find you a baby-sitter as long as you let them know in advance. Alternatively, you may prefer to make a private arrangement with a member of the staff.

If your children stray off, they are most likely to be well cared for. Contact the police.

CIGARETTES, CIGARS, TOBACCO*. International brands of cigarettes made in Jamaica are on sale in hotel shops, supermarkets and at pharmacies. This tobacco-growing country produces a limited selection of cigars of its own; some foreign makes are also available. If you are particularly attached to your own brand of pipe tobacco, bring a supply with you as you may not find it here.

Smoking is prohibited in theatres, banks, post offices and on buses, but allowed in cinemas.

CLOTHING. Informality is the rule, and during the day it's swimsuits and shorts—though you should cover up a little to go on the street. Hats are essential against the powerful sun—you can buy ideal broad-brimmed ones on the spot. A light wrap or sweater is advisable in case the breeze freshens. For a trip into the mountains, make sure you have a sweater or jacket, as well as stout walking shoes.

Evening wear is generally quite casual, though some hotels, especially in Montego Bay, require men to wear jacket and tie at dinner. Women will have the chance to wear long dresses.

COMMUNICATIONS. The postal services are generally reliable. It's advisable to have mail sent care of your hotel rather than poste restante (general delivery). For outgoing mail and inland telegrams, it's easiest—and very efficient—to use your hotel reception desk. Otherwise go to the post office. Make sure your postage is correct and that you clearly mark objects you wish airmailed: understamped letters and parcels are sent by sea and take weeks to arrive at their destination.

111

C Street mailboxes are painted either red or blue and are clearly marked LETTERBOX.

Telegrams. Domestic telegrams will be handled by your hotel. There they will usually be able to send international cables also, but if not, go to one of the offices of Jamintel (Jamaica International Telecommunications Ltd.), with branches at:

15 North Street, Kingston; tel. 922-6330
36 Fort Street, Montego Bay; tel. 952-4402

This company is also responsible for international telex and fax services. Letter telegrams, or night letters (with minimum 22 words), are half the ordinary rate.

Telephone. Jamaican telephone numbers need a little explaining, because they aren't exactly what they may seem to the uninitiated. In the telephone directory, numbers are given in a group of three digits—dash—four digits. The Kingston headquarters of the Jamaica Tourist Board, for example, is 929-9200/19. The first two digits (92) are the area code, the last five, the subscriber number. To get the Kingston number outside of town, you must dial 0 first, i.e., 0 929-9200/19.
For calls to the U.S., some parts of Jamaica are linked to the direct dialling system. Otherwise, dial 113 for the international operator. Outgoing foreign calls are subject to a 50% government tax. Reversed-charge (collect) calls can be made to Britain, the U.S.A., Canada and a limited number of other countries. Ask 113 for information.

   Public telephones, usually of the plastic-bubble type, are found on the street.

COMPLAINTS. First make any complaint to the person in charge of the establishment in question: the manager of the hotel, the head waiter in a restaurant, etc. If you feel the matter warrants it, contact the Visitors' Service Bureau of the Jamaica Tourist Board in the resorts or at the international airports. They will also be interested in receiving suggestions for improvements.

CONVERTER CHARTS. In 1978, Jamaica began the changeover from the Imperial system to the International System of Units (SI units). Length and distance are measured in metres and kilometres, volume in litres, weight in grammes and kilos and temperatures in degrees centigrade (properly called Celsius). In practice, some of the old ways linger on, and you are still likely to find distances given in miles.

Temperature

°C
°F

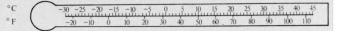

Length

cm
inches
metres
ft./yd.

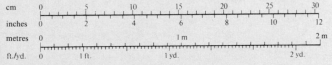

Weight

grams
ounces

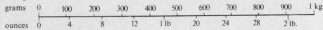

Fluid measures

imp. gals.
litres
U.S. gals.

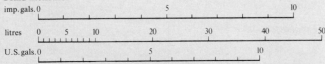

For distance measures, see page 116.

CRIME. Security patrols are vigilant in tourist areas, and just as you would steer clear of dangerous sections in New York or London, do the same in the cities of Jamaica. Keep away from the south-west districts of Kingston—the sensitive slum areas of Jones Town, Denham Town, Trench Town and Greenwich Town. Jamaicans themselves do not wander about casually here. And don't roam along the beaches after dark. For your peace of mind, double-lock your room and deposit valuables in the hotel safe. See also DRUGS.

CUSTOMS and ENTRY REGULATIONS. Nationals of Britain, most Commonwealth countries, Japan and most European countries must present valid passports—but no visas—to enter Jamaica as tourists. Americans and Canadians need no passports, but must present proof of citizenship in the form of birth certificate, voter's registration card or documents establishing legal residence, at least one with photo for identification. All visitors must also be in possession of a return or onward ticket from Jamaica and be carrying adequate funds. You will be asked to fill in a tourist card on the basis of which the permitted length of stay will be determined. Maximum length of stay: North America, 6 months; U.K., Europe and Commonwealth, 3 months, Japan 30 days.

Note: travellers (except Canadian citizens) planning a transit stop in the United States will require a visa for that country.

No vaccinations are required unless you are arriving from or have recently visited countries infected with certain serious diseases (cholera, yellow fever, etc.). In case of doubt, consult a travel agent well in advance of your departure date.

Customs formalities are kept to a minimum. The following chart shows the duty-free items you may take into Jamaica and, when returning home, into your own country:

Into:	Cigarettes	Cigars	Tobacco	Spirits	Wine
Jamaica	200	or 50	or ½ lb.	1 qt. and 1 qt.	
Australia	200	or 250 g.	or 250 g.	1 l.	or 1 l.
Canada	200	and 50	and 900 g.	1.1 l.	or 1.1 l.
Eire	200	or 50	or 250 g.	1 l.	and 2 l.
N. Zealand	200	or 50	or ½ lb.	1 qt. and 1 qt.	
U.K.	200	or 50	or 250 g.	1 l.	and 2 l.
U.S.A.	200	and 100	and *	1 l.	or 1 l.
* a reasonable quantity					

No firearms of any kind are allowed into Jamaica.

Currency restrictions. You are not permitted to bring in or take out Jamaican currency. There is no restriction on the import of foreign currency (or traveller's cheques), provided it is declared upon arrival. See also MONEY MATTERS.

D **DIPLOMATIC REPRESENTATION**

Canada   High Commission, Royal Bank (Jamaica) Ltd. Building, 30 Knutsford Boulevard, Kingston 5; tel. 926-1500

| United Kingdom | High Commission, 26 Trafalgar Road, Kingston 10; tel. 926-9050 |
| U.S.A. | Embassy, Jamaica Mutual Life Centre, 3rd Floor, 2 Oxford Road, Kingston 5; tel. 929-4850 |

For other embassies or Commonwealth high commissions, consult the telephone directory.

DRIVING IN JAMAICA. Your home driving licence is valid in Jamaica. If you are coming to the island for a relatively long stay and want to bring your own car along, plan well ahead. You must obtain a permit from the Trade Administrator's Office, which may take up to three months to come through. A bond, refundable when the vehicle leaves Jamaica, must be posted. The car can remain on the island for six months without the payment of customs duty. It may not be sold during this period.

Driving conditions: Remember to drive on the *left*. Road signs are, in the main, international. Wearing seat belts is not compulsory, but recommended. Speed limits are 30 miles per hour (50 kilometres per hour) in towns and built-up areas and 50 m.p.h. (80 k.p.h.) elsewhere, and radar checks are operated. It is wise to keep speeds down in any case, especially in the immediate vicinity of small towns and villages, because of pedestrians and animals encountered in the sometimes narrow roadway. Be prepared, also, for the often zippy local drivers, and the clouds of dust likely to be raised by buses and trucks.

If heading away from the major roads, a call to the Jamaica Tourist Board will give you a rundown on road conditions—a wise precaution following heavy rainfall. Horns are not blown at night, except when necessary.

Service stations are found in all towns. In case of breakdowns, phone your rental agency for assistance.

Parking: Meters are found in the larger cities, and parking lots are common. When you park, remove all valuables from your car and lock it.

Distances: The following chart will help you plan your excursions. Distances between certain key points are given in both miles (normal type) and kilometres *(italics)*.

D

	Kingston	Mandeville	Montego Bay	Negril	Ocho Rios	Port Antonio
Kingston		61 *98*	119 *190*	151 *242*	55 *88*	61 *98*
Mandeville	61 *98*		71 *114*	90 *144*	69 *110*	117 *187*
Montego Bay	119 *190*	71 *114*		51 *82*	64 *102*	132 *211*
Negril	151 *242*	90 *144*	51 *82*		116 *186*	182 *291*
Ocho Rios	55 *88*	69 *110*	64 *102*	116 *186*		68 *109*
Port Antonio	61 *98*	117 *187*	132 *211*	182 *291*	68 *109*	

Distance

```
km    0    1   2   3   4   5   6     8      10      12      14      16
miles 0   ½   1  1½   2       3      4      5      6      7      8      9      10
```

DRUGS. Marijuana is grown in quantity, and its use enters into Jamaica's folklore and the Rastafarian religion. Despite this, marijuana and other narcotics are illegal under Jamaican law. Though you will almost certainly, at some point, be offered *ganja* (as marijuana is known locally) by sidewalk dealers, be warned that you risk arrest, prosecution and imprisonment. Psilocybin mushrooms in any form induce dangerous hallucinations and should be avoided.

E **ELECTRIC CURRENT.** The standard power supply is 110–120 volts, 50 cycles A.C., though some hotels may be on 220 V. Refer to your hotel brochure before plugging in and, if necessary, a transformer will be provided. Since local power outlets may not be compatible with your appliance plugs, bring a spare socket from home, buy a Jamaican plug on the spot, and have the two wired up by an electrician, thus creating your own plug adaptor.

EMERGENCIES. Depending on the problem, refer to the separate entries in this section (DIPLOMATIC REPRESENTATIONS, HEALTH AND HAZARDS etc.). Hotel staff will be your greatest immediate help.

Uniform emergency telephone numbers throughout the island:

Police	119
Ambulance	110
Fire	110

GUIDES. Guided tours operate from almost all hotels, which usually have a special desk for making arrangements. All tours offered by authorized firms are accompanied. If you need a guide for private sightseeing visits, inquire at the hotel desk or contact the Jamaica Tourist Board. Many Jamaican taxi drivers are also knowledgeable guides. Your hotel receptionist will be able to recommend someone qualified for your purposes.

HEALTH and HAZARDS. To be completely at ease, take out a spe- cial health insurance through your regular insurance agent or travel firm at home to cover the risk of illness and accident while on holiday.

All major hotels have a doctor on call, and many employ a trained nurse capable of attending to minor ills. Sanitation in resort areas is good, and the public health service is vigilant.

Stomach upsets are almost certain to be due to the various changes a trip abroad brings with it: an unaccustomed diet and water mineral content, disruption of the habitual 24-hour cycle (jet-lag), nervous tension and an over-indulgence in food and drink. To begin with, take it easy on the exotica—and the rum. And include some diarrhoea tablets in your first-aid kit.

Visiting palefaces are all too likely to overexpose themselves to Jamaica's tropical sun, with the painful results that can ruin a holiday. Elementary precautions: invest in some adequate sunscreen lotion, protect your head with a broad-brimmed beach-hat and your eyes with efficient sunglasses, and dose your sunbathing for the first few days. Remember that in these latitudes you'll get brown even in the shade.

Mongooses have taken care of the snakes (there are scarcely any left outside the plantations). Mosquitoes are generally not a problem, though if need be, you can buy a spray locally. However, the beaches, especially at sundown, may attract midges which can nip you to distraction if you don't use an insect repellent (available in hotel shops, supermarkets and pharmacies). Swimmers should watch out for sea-urchins which can inflict some nasty wounds. If you accidentally step on one, the best cure is to apply lime or lemon juice immediately. This helps to calcify the spines, which then work their way harmlessly out of the skin. Razor-sharp coral can pierce your skin in an instant, so wear tennis shoes or flippers when snorkelling. Treat coral cuts as you would any wound, with antiseptic, plus the healing power of fresh sea air.

It is only common sense never to swim alone, and advisable not to go hiking alone.

HITCH-HIKING. Hitch-hiking is discouraged for visitors. If you are driving you may see someone by the side of the road making an abrupt downward gesture with the whole arm. This unfamiliar signal looks as though it should mean "go away", but it is actually a request for a lift. Use the discretion you would normally apply to picking up a passenger, especially after nightfall.

HOURS (for banking hours, see under MONEY MATTERS). Opening hours are on the whole as indicated below, though some tourist-oriented establishments keep longer hours. Virtually everything shuts down on Sundays and public holidays.

Shops. 9 or 10 a.m. to 4.30 or 5 p.m., Monday–Saturday, with variable half-day closing one day per week (e.g. Wednesday afternoons in Kingston, Thursday afternoons in Montego Bay).

Jamaica Tourist Board offices. 8.30 a.m. to 4.30 p.m., Monday–Friday.

Offices. 8.30 a.m. to 4.30 p.m., Monday–Friday, almost always closed on Saturdays.

Museums. 9. a.m. to 4.30 p.m., Monday–Saturday.

See also PUBLIC HOLIDAYS.

LANGUAGE. The official language spoken in Jamaica is English, and, as a visitor, you'll have no problems in your daily contacts with Jamaicans, despite the presence of some words and expressions that

may be unfamiliar. However, creole is the Jamaicans' *real* mother tongue, and you'll be hard put to pick out more than a few words to begin with: colourful and expressive, it's the end-result of a mixture of West African, Spanish, Indian, Chinese, French and Dutch terms on a superstructure of English.

A few examples to get the flavour:

boonoonoonoos	pleasing, charming
labrish	discussion
nyam	eat
oonou	you
talawah	brave

One traditional Jamaican saying goes: "Howdy and tenky no bruck no square." ("How d'ye do and thank you break no bones.") In other words: "It is not only good manners to be polite, but it does no harm."

LAUNDRY and DRY-CLEANING. Some hotels offer same-day service, provided you arrange to have the garments collected early enough. Otherwise, count on 24 or even 48 hours. Local firms in town take longer but apply lower rates.

LEGAL ASSISTANCE. Should you be involved in any serious accident or incident, especially one involving injury, get hold of a lawyer as quickly as possible. Your diplomatic representative may be able to advise you regarding local lawyers.

LOST PROPERTY. Check with your hotel reception desk or the establishment where you think you may have lost the article. Then, if the occasion warrants, report the loss to the police.

MAPS. Maps are featured in hotel and publicity brochures as well as in *The Gleaner's Tourist Guide*, a newspaper brought out specially for visitors and available free in most hotels. Car rental firms provide free maps for clients. The Jamaica Tourist Board sells more detailed, reliable maps at nominal prices. These are also on sale in gift and book shops.

M **MEETING PEOPLE.** Most Jamaicans have a naturally courteous and spontaneous approach to each other and to visitors. And they take the time to enjoy life; don't try to push a Jamaican around—impatience on your part would be more of a hindrance than help.

The *Meet the People Programme,* a successful scheme organized by the Jamaica Tourist Board, gives you a chance to meet islanders with interests related to yours—anything from raising a family to bird-watching, stamp-collecting, classical music or dominoes. More than 700 Jamaican families currently participate in the programme. Sometimes, small visiting cultural or sports groups can be put in touch with similar associations.

And if you've set your hearts on a tropical wedding, all you'll need to tie the knot here is 24 hours' residence on the island and permission from the Ministry of Justice in Kingston. If you feel like matching your veil to a bikini and getting married in the sea, that can be arranged, too.

A word on vocabulary. We are all natives of a country, but we don't appreciate being referred to as "natives". Nor do Jamaicans. They are "Jamaicans".

MONEY MATTERS

Currency. Gone are the nostalgic days of pounds, shillings and pence in this former British colony. In 1969, the Jamaican dollar (J$), divided into 100 cents, was introduced. Banknotes, bearing portraits of Jamaican national heroes, come in denominations of J$1, 2, 5, 10, 20 and 100. Coins of 1, 5, 10, 20, 25 and 50¢ feature the Jamaican coat-of-arms and other local motifs.

For currency restrictions, see CUSTOMS AND ENTRY REGULATIONS.

Banking hours. 9 a.m. to 2 p.m. Monday–Thursday, 9 a.m. to 12 noon and 2.30 to 5 p.m. on Fridays.

Changing money. The Jamaican dollar is the only legal tender in the island, and all bills must be settled in local currency. Visitors are asked to convert their currencies at commercial banks or exchange bureaus located at both international airports, cruise-ship piers and in nearly all hotels. Tellers must give a receipt for money converted, and you must keep this receipt to enable reconversion of Jamaican dollars to hard currency at the time of departure.

Traveller's cheques and credit cards. Traveller's cheques should preferably be in U.S. dollars; they are practically as good as cash in tourist-related circumstances. It is certainly safer to hold your holiday funds in cheques, which can be reclaimed if lost, rather than in cash. It's a good idea to follow instructions given for recording where and when you changed each cheque.

Major credit cards are widely honoured, especially by hotels, restaurants and rent-a-car firms.

NEWSPAPERS and MAGAZINES. American newspapers and magazines are usually on sale at hotel and airport news-stands; British papers can be found occasionally. And for an insight into Jamaican news and views, buy one of the local dailies. English-language paperbacks are widely available. For information on entertainment and events, pick up a copy of the *Daily Gleaner* at your hotel or at a drugstore or supermarket.

PHOTOGRAPHY. You'll probably prefer to bring a supply of film with you—certain brands are unavailable, and supplies tend to be uncertain. It's advisable to take exposed rolls home for developing.

Photography is prohibited near military installations, and there are restrictions in art galleries (though you will often be granted permission if you ask). As for snapping photogenic individuals, it's only polite to ask their permission beforehand. Some will agree, some will ask for money, some may ask for a copy of the picture, others will refuse.

Because of the strong sun and glare from sea and sand, filters are almost essential. Mornings and late afternoons are the best times for taking pictures.

Airport X-ray machines do not ruin film, but for safety's sake, put it in a bag to be examined separately by the checkers.

POLICE. The helpful and courteous Jamaican police (both male and female) wear navy trousers or skirts and matching caps with a red band. Identification is clearly displayed on their shirts. Police dressed in khaki are inspectors.

Security guards are posted in all main hotels and the grounds are patrolled at night. There are also plain-clothes police, called detectives. Members of the Jamaica Tourist Board's courtesy unit are on duty round the clock in all resort areas. All are members of

P the special police force with powers to arrest, and they are in constant contact with the regular police. They are also specially trained to assist and advise visitors, give accurate directions and other information.

PUBLIC HOLIDAYS

January 1	New Year's Day
May 23	National Labour Day
December 25	Christmas Day
December 26	Boxing Day

If these dates fall on a Saturday or Sunday, shops and offices close the following Monday.

Movable Dates	Ash Wednesday
	Good Friday
	Easter Monday
	Independence Day
	(first Monday in Aug.)
	National Heroes' Day
	(third Monday in Oct.)

R **RADIO and TV.** Jamaica's two radio stations (AM and FM) will keep you up to date on local and world events. After dark, stations all round the world can be picked up on short wave. The nation has one television station, JBC TV. All broadcasting is government-run.

Radio hams note that there are about 30 transmitting members on the island. Headquarters is:

The Jamaica Amateur Radio Association, Red Cross Building, 70 Arnold Road, Kingston 5; telephone 926-7246

RELIGIOUS SERVICES. The Jamaican constitution guarantees freedom of religion. Christian congregations—the majority—include Anglican, Baptist, Methodist, Roman Catholic and United Church (Presbyterian and Congregational). There are also Jewish, Hindu, Moslem and Bahai communities. Refer to local newspapers for addresses and times of services. The Rastafarian cult, which has followers in London, New York and elsewhere in the Caribbean, originated in Jamaica.

RESORTS. Here's a rapid rundown of the principal tourist developments on the island:

The current "in" place is **Negril** at the western tip of the island. A favourite with the young crowd.

Montego Bay in the north-west is a fully developed area ideal for swingers and night-birds.

Ocho Rios in the centre of the north coast is a good all-round resort with something for most tastes.

Occupying a magnificent natural site, **Port Antonio** over at the eastern end of the island is a relatively unspoilt area for visitors seeking tranquillity rather than kicks.

Inland **Mandeville,** at about 2,000 feet, will appeal to those who prefer a more temperate climate.

TIME DIFFERENCES. Jamaica time year-round is Eastern Standard Time, 5 hours behind GMT. The following chart shows the time in January in some selected cities. In March/April, when British and U.S. clocks advance one hour, Jamaica stays the same.

Los Angeles	Chicago	New York	**Jamaica**	London
9 a.m.	11 a.m.	noon	**noon**	5 p.m.

Dial 117 for a time check.

TIPPING

Hotel porter, per bag	J$ 1–2
Hotel maid, per week	J$ 25
Bellboy, errand	J$ 1–2
Waiter	10–15% (if not included)
Taxi driver	10%
Filling station attendant	J$ 2–3
Hairdresser/Barber	10–15%

T **TOILETS.** Tourist facilities are generally well maintained. When you are away from your hotel, use those in restaurants, petrol stations or tourist-orientated establishments.

TOURIST INFORMATION OFFICES. The Jamaica Tourist Board maintains offices in a number of countries, including:

Canada	1 Eglinton Avenue East, Suite 16, Toronto, Ont. M4P 3A1; tel. (416) 482-7850
	Mezzanine Level, 1110 Sherbrooke Street West, Montreal, Que. H3A 1G9; tel. (514) 849-6386/7
United Kingdom	63 St. James's Street, London SW1A 1LX; tel. (01) 499-1707/8
U.S.A.	36 South Wabash Avenue, Suite 1210, Chicago, IL 60603; tel. (312) 346-1546
	8411 Preston Road, Suite 605, LB31, Dallas, TX 75225; tel. (214) 361-8778
	3440 Wilshire Boulevard, Suite 1207, Los Angeles, CA 90010; tel. (213) 384-1123
	1320 South Dixie Highway, Suite 1100, Coral Gables, Miami, FL 33146; tel. (305) 665-0557
	866 Second Avenue, 10th Floor, New York, NY 10017; tel. (212) 688-7650

Headquarters of the Jamaica Tourist Board is in the Tourism Centre: 21 Dominica Drive, New Kingston, Kingston 5; tel. (809) 929-9200/19; telex 2140, fax (809) 929-9375

There are offices at both Kingston and Montego Bay international airports, as well as in the following towns:

Mandeville	21 Ward Avenue; tel. 962-1072
Montego Bay	Cornwall Beach; tel. 952-4425
Negril	Plaza de Negril, Negril P.O.; tel. 957-4243
Ocho Rios	Ocean Village Shopping Centre; tel. 974-2570
Port Antonio	City Centre Plaza; tel. 993-3051

TRANSPORT (see also CAR HIRE)

Taxis*. Taxis in Jamaica do not have meters. Best to ask your hotel to

call a cab for you or to agree on the fare before engaging the vehicle.

T

There are special buses and taxis which serve the tourist industry. They are members of JUTA and offer point-to-point services at fixed rates.

Between midnight and 5 a.m. a surcharge is added to the fare. It is customary to tip the driver (see TIPPING).

Buses. Both town and country buses are rather infrequent and usually overcrowded.

Limousines. Less expensive than taxis, limousine transport from airport to hotel is often included in package deals.

Trains*. Diesel trains run between Kingston and Montego Bay, taking about 4½ hours each way. It's a nice, leisurely way of seeing the real Jamaica away from the tourist spots. Pedlars come aboard, and small country markets enliven the scene along the track. There are also more luxurious tourist rail tours such as the Governor's Coach and the Appleton Express that run through the Cockpit Country (see pp. 45–46).

Local air services. Trans Jamaican Airlines operates daily flights between Kingston, Port Antonio, Ocho Rios, Montego Bay, Negril and Mandeville. The domestic airport in Kingston is Tinson Pen.

Air taxis fly to a larger number of points across the island.

Regional Caribbean air services. Island-hopping aircraft of intercontinental and regional carriers will transport you to Haiti, the Cayman Islands and virtually every other nook and cranny of the great arc of the Antilles. Remember to confirm all flights 72 hours in advance.

Rafts. For a complete change of pace, put on your swimsuit and clamber aboard a bamboo raft for a romantic voyage down the Rio Grande, Great or Martha Brae rivers. Your hotel tour desk can make the arrangements for this uniquely Jamaican experience. Wearing a bathing suit is fine, but not necessary unless you plan to swim. However, your feet will get wet, so best avoid socks or stockings.

WATER. In towns and hotels piped water, including that in drinking fountains, is chlorinated, filtered and completely safe to drink. Very rarely, in out-of-the-way places, you may come across untreated supplies, which are clearly indicated as such. Do not drink from rivers or streams. Bottled water (carbonated only) is available, and you may, of course, like to purchase water-purifying tablets from your pharmacy at home just in case.

W

125

Index

An asterisk (*) next to a page number indicates a map reference. For index to Practical Information, see inside front cover.

INDEX

09 8/910 RPC 11